Praise for *The Hidden POWER of Your Past Lives*

"Through this book, Sandra gives us an understanding of why we've made certain choices in our life, based on our past lives. She shows us how we can break cycles and live the life that we want. This is a remarkably eye-opening book that will make you think about the journey you're on."

— **Lisa Williams**, the best-selling author of *The Survival of the Soul*

*"Sandra Anne Taylor is a rare genius and one of the most remarkable women on the planet today. In **The Hidden Power of Your Past Lives,** she reminds you that the opposite of death is birth and that there's no opposite to life. Rather, there's a continuum from physical life to nonphysical life and back again. Through decades of strong focus and conscious living, Sandra has brought forth a deeply insightful body of work that offers meaning to so many unanswered questions. I enthusiastically endorse her teachings—there is much to learn here."*

— **Dr. Darren R. Weissman**, the best-selling author of *Awakening to the Secret Code of Your Mind*

*"**The Hidden Power of Your Past Lives** is a powerful tool for healing and success and a truly unique approach to the subject of reincarnation. Sandra Anne Taylor's rare insights, techniques, and affirmations can free readers from old blocks and attachments and lift them to a wonderful new future that has long been buried in the past."*

— **Colette Baron-Reid**, the best-selling author of *The Map*

"If the soul evolves through many lifetimes, **The Hidden Power of Your Past Lives** is a great user's manual for this stop on the journey. Not just a metaphysical treatise on reincarnation, the book is a practical and sophisticated guide for using an understanding of past lives to transform the deep coding that shapes your current life."

— **Donna Eden**, the best-selling author of *Energy Medicine*

"Along the way, there's content that advances your spiritual realization in one quantum burst. Sandra Anne Taylor's new book, **The Hidden Power of Your Past Lives**, possesses exactly this content.

"I've studied philosophy and religion most of my life. During my adventure, I've looked into many paths and secret societies and even served at the highest of levels in ancient orders, all in my quest to become enlightened. Common to almost all of this work is the understanding generally referred to as reincarnation. Even the Christian tradition is full of references that can only be to past lives.

"With this background, I must admit that I've never read anything as clear and cogent as Sandra's distilled teachings from her many years of research and collaboration on the subject. Deep within your subconscious mind exists information that propels you. Whether you think past lives are real or not, you'll want to read this book for the power and insight gained from this perspective."

— **Eldon Taylor**, the best-selling author of
Choices and Illusions and *Mind Programming*

"Could the key to life's mysteries be hidden in the plain sight of everyday living? Sandra Anne Taylor believes so, and in her new book **The Hidden Power of Your Past Lives**, she gives us good reasons to believe so as well.

"In a riveting journey of case histories and personal revelations, she demonstrates how everything from the healing of our bodies to the success of our relationships is often linked to experiences from the past. If her ideas are right, they catapult us light years beyond conventional explanations of the seemingly meaningless events in life. One thing is certain: there's something missing in the traditional story of why things 'are' as they are, and only new thinking will reveal the missing link of our soul's meaning and purpose.

"Whether you're an artist or an engineer, this book is about you, your world, and every relationship that you'll ever experience in life."

— **Gregg Braden,** the best-selling author of
The Divine Matrix and *Fractal Time*

The Hidden
POWER
of Your Past Lives

The Hidden
POWER
of Your Past Lives

REVEALING YOUR
ENCODED CONSCIOUSNESS

Sandra Anne Taylor

HAY HOUSE, INC.
Carlsbad, California • New York City
London • Sydney • Johannesburg
Vancouver • Hong Kong • New Delhi

Published and distributed in the United States by: Hay House, Inc.: www.hayhouse.com • *Published and distributed in Australia by:* Hay House Australia Pty. Ltd.: www.hayhouse .com.au • *Published and distributed in the United Kingdom by:* Hay House UK, Ltd.: www .hayhouse.co.uk • *Published and distributed in the Republic of South Africa by:* Hay House SA (Pty), Ltd.: www.hayhouse.co.za • *Distributed in Canada by:* Raincoast Books: www.raincoast .com • *Published in India by:* Hay House Publishers India: www.hayhouse.co.in

Editorial supervision: Jill Kramer   •   *Project editor:* Jessica Kelley
Cover design: Christy Salinas   •   *Interior design:* Tricia Breidenthal

Chapters by Tom Cratsley and Sharon A. Klingler used with permission.

Library of Congress Cataloging-in-Publication Data

Taylor, Sandra Anne.
  The hidden power of your past lives : revealing your encoded consciousness / Sandra Anne Taylor. -- 1st ed.
    p. cm.
  ISBN 978-1-4019-2901-5 (hardcover : alk. paper) 1. Reincarnation. I. Title.
  BP573.R5T39 2011
  133.901'35--dc23
                                 2011017834

ISBN: 978-1-4019-4542-8
Digital ISBN: 978-1-4019-2902-2

17 16 15 14   7 6 5 4
1st edition, October 2011
4th edition, May 2014

Printed in the United States of America

With love to my precious grandson,
Ethan Mikhail Taylor.
And to you, the reader—we are connected now
and surely have been in the past!

❋ CONTENTS ❋

PART III: Releasing the Past, Healing the Present, and
Freeing the Future!

✻ INTRODUCTION ✻

I'm very excited about beginning this adventure into past-life exploration with you. Those who are familiar with my other books might consider this a departure for me, but that's not the case, since I've been teaching classes about the energy of reincarnation for decades. And while this concept may not seem to fit with the themes of attraction and destiny creation, which dominate my previous work, they're all intrinsically connected.

All of my books have been centered around the application of quantum physics to the human experience, and this one is no different. Although reincarnation doesn't seem to be a very scientific principle, the elements of energy, consciousness, and time are actually supremely applicable to this subject.

For years I've investigated how the elements of human awareness and energy influence our destiny creation. A lot of concepts, such as consciousness-created reality, seem to lay down clear-cut connections between the causes and effects of what we attract. In terms of energy, there are so many things from our present lives—including our thoughts, emotions, beliefs, and choices—that influence the people and situations we draw to us, but it doesn't stop there.

While I was researching my most recent book, *Truth, Triumph, and Transformation,* I realized that there were still a lot of unknowns. It seemed that difficult things were happening to people for no apparent reason, and I'd have to dig deeper to find the answers. I needed to address the importance of past-life influences on the issue of attraction.

Of course, not all of our difficult events are sourced in previous incarnations. Other factors, such as spirit cycles, soul lessons, and shared consciousness, are also vital factors, which I did discuss in my last book. But a hugely powerful—yet virtually unknown—influence had to be the encoded energies of our earlier lives.

Since your consciousness preexisted this embodiment, your accumulated past-life information is a compelling piece of your destiny creation. Your present is an extension of your past; and with every lifetime, new information is encoded. You've brought your karma code into this existence; and although the details may be hidden to you at this point, they're still significant factors in what's going on at this very moment.

But you no longer have to stay unaware of these elements in your destiny creation. The processes on the CD accompanying this book are designed to bring past-life facts into your consciousness, to release the emotions and conclusions that may be lingering, and to heal and rescript your karma code. They're easy, self-guided meditations that can be used at your leisure to make these important investigations and changes.

I recommend that you read the entire book before listening to the CD. For a thorough explanation of each process, I suggest you read Chapter 11 in its entirety before doing the guided meditations. Please don't listen to the recording while you're driving or engaged in any activity that demands your focused awareness. These exercises serve an important purpose, and your attention should be directed to the meditative process.

I also recommend that you keep a journal to help with your past-life investigation. There are many places throughout the book where I ask exploratory questions. Answer them in your journal and write down all your impressions. It's also a good idea to keep the notebook by your bed, for once you start this journey, you'll find that you get bits and pieces of information in your dreams and meditations that apply to these past-life experiences.

As I mentioned, I've been teaching classes on reincarnation for nearly 30 years. I owe my introduction to the subject to Edgar Cayce and the profound material from his readings. People wrote to him for help with healing; and in his trance state, he identified the past-life traumas involved. His work on karma and the reincarnation process has been illuminating for me.

In my early years, I took many extensive seminars from the Association for Research and Enlightenment (ARE), part of the Edgar Cayce Foundation. Some of the theories you find in this book were presented in those seminars and postulated in the readings of Edgar Cayce long ago. I'm grateful for these resources, and I recommend the Cayce books on karma and reincarnation for those who want to delve further into this fascinating subject.

I also want to introduce my two contributors, Tom Cratsley and Sharon A. Klingler, who have graciously contributed to this book and who have also been inestimably helpful throughout my life.

Tom Cratsley, who designed a powerful restructuring process for dealing with past trauma, has contributed Chapter 8: Deconstructing Misery, Reconstructing Joy. For the past 10 years, Tom has been the Assistant Director of the Fellowships of the Spirit School of Spiritual Healing and Prophecy in Cassadaga, New York. He has studied psychology and religion at Harvard Divinity School and is a certified hypnotherapist and remarkable healer. Tom can be contacted at Harmony House in Lily Dale, New York, or through **www.tomcratsley.com**.

Sharon A. Klingler, who wrote Chapter 10: Getting to Know Your Past-Life Guides, is an internationally renowned medium and teacher who has authored several books and audio programs on the subject of connecting with Spirit. These include *Intuition & Beyond, Life with Spirit,* the *Speaking to Spirit* program, and many CDs. You can contact Sharon at **www.starbringerassociates.com**.

In addition, I want to thank Donna Eden and David Feinstein, whose work I refer to in Chapter 11. In my search for tools that are especially helpful for clearing past-life codes, I've found that energy medicine and the Emotional Freedom Technique (EFT) provide significant assistance. You can learn more about these experts and the techniques they teach at **www.innersource.net**.

Karma to Come

In addition to finding out how your past relates to this life, it's also interesting to examine how your present choices will influence the future. I want to recommend that you keep this in mind when reading this book. Your clear choices now can lead to a much more liberated future, free from pesky and unwanted obstacles, and the change could be immediate and dramatic!

This reminds me of a funny story concerning the issue of future influence. My son was driving me somewhere in his car when I asked him to turn on the air-conditioning to accommodate one of the many hot flashes I've started having recently.

He said, "Are you kidding? It's cold out!"

I replied, "You'd better have some compassion for me, or next time you'll come back as a woman just to find out what this feels like."

"I'm *never* coming back as a woman!" he declared. Then he paused and looked at me. After a moment, he leaned over and turned on the air—*just in case!*

This is a lighthearted story that reveals a deep truth. Everything we do . . . all of our choices—*our love and our refusal to love, our patience and intolerance—feed our hidden code. And every important relationship does, too.* We're all interconnected—certainly energetically and often through karma—and it's endlessly fascinating to find out how our past connections are playing out now, and how our actions could be feeding the future.

For your present happiness and your destiny—both in this and in upcoming lives—it's well worth the effort and time to explore your own encoded consciousness and reveal the information that may be hidden there.

Keep in mind that karma isn't the only influence on what's happening to you today. I wrote about such factors as the psychological and spiritual influences of destiny creation in my book *Secrets of Success,* while *Quantum Success* addresses the issues of career and financial attraction, and *Secrets of Attraction* investigates the influences on romantic love.

The intention in this book, however, is to shed light on how your encoded energy from previous lifetimes can still be affecting *all* of these arenas without your even knowing it. Through the many cases I recount here—both my own and those of my clients—it becomes apparent that our unknown past experiences do have a hidden power. All of the stories are true, although the names have been changed. In every one, the search for past-life meaning has been transformative.

You, too, can decode the information that still lies hidden within, and your desire to do so will send you in a healing direction, helping you arrive at a deeper understanding and a more empowered approach to everything you do. Instead of bouncing through life simply reacting to circumstances, you can work on understanding what it all means. The present is intricately interwoven with the past in the tapestry of your encoded consciousness. When you investigate the colors and the patterns there, you'll be able to resolve difficult issues and find the meaning, healing, and fulfillment you're looking for.

"If time is just another dimension, then the entire history of the Universe from beginning to end is spread along this time line. The past still exists and so does the future. Our human perception of an eternal present which seems to travel along in the future direction is an illusion: that's not the way the world is at all."

— NICK HERBERT, *QUANTUM REALITY*

PART I

The Tides of
TIME

Chapter 1

BACK IN THE
SADDLE AGAIN . . .
AND AGAIN

What do you think happens when you die? Do you think your body turns to dust; and the intelligent, creative identity that you were just ceases to be? Or maybe you believe that your soul lives on—only to spend all of eternity in those mysterious places called heaven and hell. Or perhaps there's another alternative—one that could make a lot of sense!

The theory of reincarnation has been written about and explored for millennia and is widely accepted throughout the world—especially in the East, where it's the basis of many religious beliefs. Yet those of us in the West have come rather late to

3

the discussion. Although many people still tend to dismiss the idea out of hand, the trend is changing, and statistics now show that the concept of reincarnation has taken hold in the imagination of millions of Westerners.

If you've ever wondered about the possibility that you've been here before, take a moment to consider the following questions:

- Have you ever met someone whom you instantly felt you knew?

- Do you have a natural talent for something—perhaps in sports, language, or music—that was amazingly easy to pick up?

- Do you feel more like a parent than a partner to your spouse?

- Does it seem as though you keep running into the same old obstacles—or the same types of people— over and over again?

- Have you ever arrived at a place you've never been, yet you felt as though you knew it intimately?

- Have you ever had an immediate and unexplainable aversion to certain foods, places, or people?

- Do you have an addiction to a substance—or even a person—that seems impossible to shake?

- Have you ever felt instantly attracted to someone you just met?

If you've answered *yes* to any of these questions, the reasons could be found in past-life experiences. Your sense of familiarity with a new acquaintance or place could be a subtle memory resonating in the recesses of your eternal consciousness. A personal talent may well be the current blossoming of a past-life skill. Deep feelings of irresistible attraction might indicate unbridled passion from a previous existence. And that difficult addiction could be sourced in patterns and problems from long, long ago.

Coming Back

Your soul is eternal. Your spirit doesn't end; it merely transforms. It longs to experience life, to express itself, and to connect with other souls in the physical realm. Through these experiences, you form attachments. Relationships evolve, and personalities develop patterns of behavior and emotion.

In the never-ending consciousness that is your essence, the experiences from lifetime after lifetime tend to accumulate and create specific directions for your personal path. It becomes immensely helpful, then, to explore the past in order to understand the present and redirect your future. This process of self-discovery is endlessly interesting, and the information that comes up (both logistical and emotional) can be intensely revealing. Throughout this book, I'll discuss cases that I've dealt with personally, but for now let's take a look at a few that have been documented historically.

The Case of the *Legal* Past-Life Memory

This fascinating account was first described in William Seabrook's book *Adventures in Arabia,* published in 1927. A boy named Najib Abu Faray grew up in the mountains of Lebanon, a member of the Druze people, never leaving home till the age of 20, when he was taken to a place called Djebel Druze. Once there, he recognized everything. He knew the place from a past life, and he called it his own village. He went directly to the house that he remembered as being his, and proceeded to point out where he'd hidden a bag of money behind a wall. When the bricks were torn down, the money was there.

The boy discovered that his name had been Mansour Atrash, and he identified many family members from that incarnation. He was taken to the Atrash family vineyards where a boundary was being disputed. He clearly recalled where the property lines were set during his life as Mansour Atrash. Since he'd given so much accurate evidence of his previous identity, his testimony was actually accepted in a Druze court of law, and the boundaries were settled according to his past-life recollections.

He was embraced by the Atrash family, and an amazing fact was revealed during his visit. It turned out that Najib Abu Faray had been born in the same hour that Mansour Atrash was killed 20 years earlier. His soul had returned immediately, coming to a family of the same culture but living hundreds of miles away.

The Case of Bridey Murphy

The first popular instance of reincarnation widely known in America is that of Bridey Murphy. In this case from the early 1950s, a young woman named Virginia Tighe (called Ruth Simmons in the first published accounts) was hypnotized with the intention to recall incidents from her childhood. Although this age regression was designed to awaken memories of the early episodes of her youth, the experience didn't stop there, but went back farther than anyone had anticipated.

During the regression, Virginia suddenly started to speak in an Irish brogue, recounting details of her life as a woman called Bridey Murphy. She related several details, including the name of the school she attended and her husband's name, as well as her father-in-law's name and profession. She also provided very specific information about the lifestyle, food, and music common to

Ireland in the mid-1800s. She named people she interacted with, such as her grocer, as well as the specific locations in the area of Cork where she'd resided.

Subsequent investigation showed that much of what Virginia "remembered" was verifiable, even the grocer's name and her father-in-law's profession. In addition, the vocabulary and terminology she used while in regression proved to be correct. Some people believed she could have gotten this information by means other than past-life memory, and both sides of this fascinating case were discussed in Morey Bernstein's 1956 book, *The Search for Bridey Murphy*. Although the belief in reincarnation was pervasive in many parts of the world at that time, this was a new concept for Americans, and the book took the country by storm. People were surprised to find out how many world religions and philosophies supported the theory. In fact, it even appears in the Bible.

Jesus, John, and Elijah

In the Old Testament it was prophesied that Elijah (also called Elias) would come to prepare the way for the Messiah—that he would be reborn at the time of the coming of the savior. Jesus refers to the prediction of the prophet's return in Matthew 17:10–13:

And his disciples asked him, saying: why then say the scribes that Elias must first come?

And Jesus answered and said unto them, Elias truly shall first come, and restore all things.

But I say unto you, that Elias is come already, and they knew him not, but have done unto him whatever they listed. Likewise shall also the Son of man suffer of them.

For the disciples understood that he spoke unto them of John the Baptist.

At other points in Matthew (11:7–9, 14–15) Jesus refers to John the Baptist by name and specifically identifies him as the reincarnation of Elias:

And as they departed, Jesus began to say unto the multitudes concerning John, what went ye out into the wilderness to see? A reed shaken with wind? . . .

But what went ye out for to see? A prophet? Yes, I say unto you, and more than a prophet. For this is he, of whom it is written. Behold, I send my messenger before thy face, which shall · prepare the way before thee. . . .

And if you will receive it, this is Elias, which was for to come.

He that hath ears to hear, let him hear.

The meaning of both these biblical excerpts is clear. Jesus is talking about the earthly return of the prophet Elijah, who'd lived hundreds of years earlier. He very clearly references John the Baptist throughout these and other verses, identifying him as Elias, a reembodiment of the prophet whose coming was foretold to pave the way for the Messiah.

While it may be surprising to some that Jesus himself spoke of the phenomenon of reincarnation, this philosophy was actually quite common among Jews of that time, as revealed by the famous Jewish historian Flavius Josephus. He meticulously detailed the life, times, politics, and philosophies of that period, writing:

> The bodies of all men are indeed mortal . . . but the soul is ever immortal . . . the pure spirits who are in conformity with the Divine dispensation lived on in the lowliest of heavenly places, and in course of time they are again sent down to inhabit sinless bodies . . .

In Time, Space, and Parallel Universes

Moving from the ancient world to modern physics, it's becoming quite clear that the more we know, the more we realize how much we have yet to discover. The fact that the Universe is largely made up of unknown energy and unknown matter (called dark space and dark matter) is an indication of how very much we have yet to learn. It's wise, then, to keep an open mind while investigating our human connection to this vast energetic world.

One of the more recent items on the quantum physics menu is a concept known as M-theory, which states that the universe exists in 11 dimensions, with the 11th dimension being home to an untold number of parallel universes. These exist on vibrating membranes, sheets that can connect and intersect. It's possible, then, to imagine past-life events and future-life potentials on these neighboring membranes, with unlimited amounts of information stored there.

These membranes are the homes of entire universes, mysterious realms that some scientists say are no farther away than the length of our eyelashes! And although they can't be seen—or perhaps even sensed in truly conscious and present ways—they hold worlds of reality in an unknown dimension.

So what does this mean in terms of our own experience? Well, for one thing, it means that what seems to be clear, true, and predictable may not be at all. Reality isn't limited to what our physical senses can recognize and define. There are unlimited potential events that we may not even be conscious of, yet it's possible that we could become aware of these alternate realities. Because of the strange and malleable nature of time, it may be entirely possible to glimpse past or future events located on other membranes.

In this scenario, our consciousness might be able to jump from one membrane to another, just to return again to the present vibration and experience. It would be the human equivalent of the *quantum leap.* Although in recent years this term has been used as a metaphor for many different types of shifting and transformation, it was originally used to describe the random jumping of an electron from one orbit around the nucleus of an atom to another orbit. This is an apt metaphor, for it's entirely possible for our consciousness to visit other times and perhaps even other realms and return with a memory of those events.

For the most part, our awareness revolves in the orbit of our present incarnation. But we may be able to jump to the path of another life, gather information there, and bring it back to examine its relevance and importance in our present experience. Such an exploration can make a great deal of difference in the events and emotions of this life. In fact, clearing up karmic influences can change everything!

Some people argue that the expanding population is proof that karma and reincarnation can't be true. How can so many souls exist now when so few existed in the past? We have to realize that this isn't the only realm where spirits spend their time. New ones are always entering from other planes of existence. Also, many people believe that as souls develop, they may choose to split into more than one identity so that they can experience more and get much more done. This may sound strange, but in terms of our eternal power, nothing is impossible.

It Makes Sense . . .

When you consider the science of energy and matter, the continuity of life just makes sense. We know that energy doesn't just cease, and matter consistently transforms. If this is true on a cosmic level, why shouldn't it be true for our individual identities and lives?

Reincarnation also explains a lot concerning the many unanswered questions we have. For example, it's difficult to understand why some people seem to suffer more than others. Perhaps it's not as random as many think—perhaps what we perceive as hardship is merely a return of energy, an opportunity to understand something unlearned in previous lifetimes. To some, unexplained suffering might seem to be the work of a capricious and uncaring God, but when we understand the subtle nuances of karmic energy and soul lessons, things start to become much more clear. And while I don't believe that difficulty in this life is a form of karmic punishment, I do believe that current problems can refer back to historical issues.

Reincarnation could also explain all of the phenomena listed in the questions at the beginning of this chapter: the sensation that you've known a recent acquaintance for a very long time; precocious talent—be it musical, artistic, mathematic, linguistic, or athletic; love at first sight, irresistible attraction, or the inability to let go of a romantic relationship; addictions; weight problems;

phobias; birth defects; allergies; and sexual preferences. All of these things, although they may also have present-life explanations, are more thoroughly understood and make much more sense from an eternal point of view.

This past-life influence may also be a powerful, yet hidden, attraction factor. In recent years, people have been fascinated with the question of how and why they attract certain things to their lives, and lately they're wondering what's been blocking the way. While not every obstacle is based in karma, it's been amazing for me to see how many individuals have been able to shift their present stuck circumstances by addressing issues from previous existences.

My First Cases

I became convinced of the power of our past lives during my 25 years in private psychological practice. In a number of cases where I was conducting hypnotic regression to discern more details about my client's youth, the person spontaneously regressed much farther. These individuals—without intention, instruction, or any expectation whatsoever—automatically went back to a previous existence.

This is not just interesting; it can also be extremely helpful therapeutically. I stumbled upon this quite by accident when I was hypnotizing a client and experienced the first spontaneous past-life regression in a therapeutic setting. I'd been trained in many types of hypnosis, and I often used it with clients who didn't recall their early years. Preverbal and even prepubescent memory loss isn't uncommon for people who've had difficult childhoods, often acting as a protective device when someone doesn't want to remember something traumatic.

I believed this was the case when a young woman named Maxine sought therapy to treat a severe social phobia. She came to see me around the age of 15, and she hadn't been to school (or pretty much anyplace else) in at least four years. She was afraid of people, afraid of being judged, and afraid of showing anxiety symptoms in public.

Since she had no memories of anything before the age of seven, I thought there might be some episodes in childhood that would give us more specific information about the source of her problems. This, then, could help us reverse her phobic tendencies.

Upon starting the regression, Maxine immediately began to describe herself sitting on some steps: "There are very big stairs in front of a huge church with a giant dome on top."

She continued, "This is funny—how can this be? I'm older here. How can I be older than I am now? I don't know why this is happening, but this is what I see." I told her just to keep telling me about it, and to describe herself and her situation.

In that life she was seriously deformed, and she couldn't work. In order to support herself, she begged for money, waiting for worshippers who were leaving the services, hoping they'd take pity on her.

She described it this way: "People are coming out of the church, and they're laughing at me. One man with a top hat is stepping on me. He's angry, kicking my foot out of the way and calling me a nuisance."

At this point Maxine started to cry, lamenting her condition and how badly people were treating her. As these memories came pouring out, I asked her to describe how she felt and to let me know if there were any more details she could pick up. She reported that she felt ashamed and hopeless. She said that she lived nearby and also described the streets in front of the domed church, along with the neighborhood she was in—yet she had no clue where she was. In her present life, she was a 15-year-old girl from Cleveland who'd hardly left home due to her anxiety. Still, she was able to depict the strange place in great detail.

As she expanded on her description, I felt I knew the church she was talking about. Although I didn't tell her at the time, I believed she was sitting on the steps of Saint Paul's Cathedral in London, England.

After she came out of the regression, I told her to keep a journal by her bed because she might get some more images or information in her dreams. We agreed to meet again the following week, and I told her that I'd bring several pictures of different churches in case one of them rang true or stimulated more memories.

I brought in seven images, from famous cathedrals such as Sacré-Coeur in Paris and Saint Patrick's in New York to unnamed country churches, as well as a mosque and a synagogue. The last picture I showed her was of Saint Paul's Cathedral in London, England.

When Maxine saw it, she exclaimed, "That's it! That's where I lived and that's where I begged! That's where the people were mean to me—right there when I sat on those stairs."

Slowly we peeled off the hidden layers of her phobia, revealing the emotions and decoding the information. Maxine had been kicked, treated brutally, denigrated, and even spat upon. She'd felt worthless, powerless to hide her deformities and shame. These feelings were so charged that it was natural for them to become deeply encoded in her consciousness and carried into this life to be healed. Not only had she brought with her the fear of being judged, she'd also brought the belief that she needed to protect and isolate herself.

So we went back and released the toxic conclusions. We also rescripted the situation, a process that reverses the event (and which is explained in Chapter 11). We used extensive cognitive restructuring to realign Maxine's present thinking and bring real truth to her self-esteem. In addition, we used relaxation therapy and systematic desensitization to allow her to get methodical exposure to social situations, retraining her comfort level around other people.

It took a while, but in time Maxine was able to get out, start working, get her general equivalency diploma (GED), and live a healthy and happy life. I'm not sure, however, if we would have been able to effect such a complete recovery by using only the classic techniques of desensitization and cognitive and relaxation therapy. Although it wasn't my intention at the time, it was providential that her past-life information came to the surface.

Maxine felt extremely relieved. She had far less anxiety just from knowing what had happened. The truth of the experience resonated with her and answered a lot of questions. She'd had extreme anxiety throughout her life, always wondering why she felt that way and making herself faulty for it.

She certainly hadn't come in for a past-life regression, and until it happened, she didn't even believe in reincarnation. But the experience felt so real and so important in her personal evolution that it was impossible for her to dismiss. In fact, it assisted her so much in her healing process that she became interested in what information could be hiding in other past lives.

It was a new experience for me in the clinical environment, too. Although I'd been interested in reincarnation for some time,

I never felt it was appropriate to introduce it into the therapeutic setting. I did change the induction I used in my hypnosis sessions, however, to open up the potential of other such spontaneous events. I decided to let Spirit lead the way—not directing a past-life focus, but allowing it to happen of its own accord.

About a year after that first, unexpected regression with Maxine, I read what was then a new book: *Many Lives, Many Masters* by Brian L. Weiss, M.D., a courageous psychiatrist who'd fallen into some spontaneous regressions of his own. His enlightened and groundbreaking work opened the door for many serious therapists to delve more deeply into this aspect of human consciousness. From that point on, I recommended his book to my clients as a way to introduce them to the concept of past-life influence and to investigate this as a part of their own therapy.

I'll talk about these cases and about my own personal experiences throughout this book, but for now I only ask that you open your heart and mind to the possibility. It's more than just a theory to me, and as you settle in with the information and become more and more comfortable with this vital concept, I believe you'll find that it means more to you, too.

In fact, as you read this book, you may find yourself moving through unseen portals into your own past existences. You'll get glimpses of your former identities, feel emotions floating back, and begin to understand the reasons why you're experiencing the patterns and events of this, your present life. And once those reasons become clear, it will be far easier to break through the blocks and make the changes you long for. The obstacles you thought were immovable will be released, allowing you to arrive at a more peaceful, productive, and prosperous place than you may have ever thought possible.

Chapter 2

VISITING ETERNITY

Eternity . . . endless time! It's a vibration of reality that's hard to define, an expanse of infinite possibilities in a field of ongoing information. Yet as indescribable and mercurial as eternity may be, we've all been there—and more frequently than we may know. This passage through vibrational portals can occur in all sorts of ways, including our dreams.

In fact, the first time I was aware of exploring this intriguing realm was in a very elaborate and vivid dream I had when I was about 17 years old. I recall every detail, even today—partly because it was so very extraordinary, and partly because I recorded it in my journal and told practically everyone I knew. It was exciting and unusual, changing my life and starting me on a brand-new path. Here's what happened in that dream:

A man who looked like a monk, dressed in a brown robe with a rope belt, came up to me and said, "I have something to show you. Come with me."

He took my hand, and we started walking down a long road—or rather, the road was passing beneath us. As we moved forward, a blur of light and color passed by on either side.

I asked the man where he was taking me, and he said, "To the place where time does not exist."

In an instant, we were in a place made merely of light and color. We stopped and looked around, and the monk said, "This is where people come when their bodies die. This is the soul's place."

The space seemed to expand to infinity. It was filled with light as far as I could see in every direction.

Upon closer examination, I saw that there were countless individual columns of light. Some were moving from place to place. Some were vibrating differently than the others—more brightly or more expansively. And I even heard strange music that had no melody, just notes and chords in a distant kind of harmony.

I asked what the lights were doing, and the monk said, "They do what needs to be done here and elsewhere."

It was an interesting place with a busy energy, but very peaceful, too. After a few more minutes of soaking up the beautiful vibration, the man said, "There's another soul place you need to see."

We passed through the radiance and the harmony to another dimension where the columns of light were more clearly defined. I even seemed to see spheres that looked like heads on each one. The feeling here was less expansive, although like the other, I couldn't see any end to it from side to side. Instead of music, I seemed to hear countless voices, all in quiet murmurs. The lights seemed to be clustered in groups and talking to each other. Yet I knew they weren't physically speaking—nor was I hearing with my ears. It was more of an inner hearing, a sort of knowing.

The monk said, "This is where souls gather before they're reborn. They're deciding who and what they'll be to each other in their next lives." He went on to tell me that we all come back, often with the people we've been with before, and we have important purposes together.

We moved closer to one of the clustered groups, and I could feel a palpable energy of love connecting all the columns of light. I "heard" plans of adventures and good times, and I also heard them talking about the interesting lessons and challenging times ahead. Yet there was no fear, no anger, no resentment or unrest—just a sense of willingness to engage with each other and an excitement for the opportunities to come.

"We offer to teach each other lessons," the monk said. *"It's all a part of each soul's greater plan."*

My spirit friend then took me to other places, beautiful expanses filled with orbs of brilliant light. He called them "the Higher Beings," and while he didn't identify them as such, I took them to be angels and very old, wise souls—whom I now would refer to as Ascended Masters. The love and creativity that emanated from these light beings touched me deeply and made me think that I would never feel alone again.

The dream went on, and we returned to the place where people gathered before birth, stopping to listen to the conversations of many of the groups clustered there. I heard people recalling their past lives and discussing what they needed to learn this time around. In each group there was a deep sense of camaraderie, even though some of the details revealed that there could be some hostility here on the earthly plane.

After observing several groups, the monk said it was time to go back. As soon as he uttered that phrase, we were back at the beginning of the road upon which we'd started our journey.

I asked, "Why have you shown me all this?"

He replied, "You need to know. It will be very important, and it's time to start your journey now."

Then the monk disappeared, and I woke up with a start. I immediately wrote everything down.

This dream was very real to me, and even though it may seem unlikely, it happened just as I described. I saw and felt the energy of light, and although the information was strange to me at the time, I utterly believed the truths revealed to me by that tender-hearted spirit.

This represented a big shift for me. I'd gone to Catholic schools all my life and wasn't at all prepared for what I experienced that night. Reincarnation had only been a vague concept that I'd been told belonged to primitive peoples in far-off foreign countries. So I had to ask myself: *What was the meaning of this dream?*

I knew it had a purpose, one that was intrinsically connected to my own reason for being here. After that night, I started reading everything I could on theories of life after life. I took my first meditation class, and it opened up a whole new world of peace and revelation to me.

The concept of learning from previous life experiences made a lot of sense. And later when I studied the physics of energy and time, it became clear why this was a very logical and purposeful process. And then, when I had my first past-life regression a few years later, the pieces of my own puzzle started to fall into place.

Near Death and Back

Through regression and dreams, I have, on many occasions, visited timeless places since the "monk" took me on that astounding journey. The most compelling and life-changing event, however, was when I had a near-death experience.

My father had died a few years earlier, and because I was unable to accept or deal with his passing, I'd completely depleted my immune system. The condition I developed, Common Variable Immune Deficiency (CVID), caused me to be prone to chronic infections, some of which were so virulent that they were totally debilitating. For six months straight, I experienced a terrible virus that inflamed my lungs and gave me ongoing asthma and sinus problems.

It was a serious condition, and I hadn't realized that it was related to internalizing my grief and rage over my father's death. (In my last book, *Truth, Triumph, and Transformation,* I wrote about the need to release deep and difficult feelings in order to stay healthy, as well as to project a truly magnetic life-force energy. If you think that ignoring difficult experiences will make your energy more positive, think again. I nearly died doing that.)

Because of that ongoing bronchial infection, I thought I'd have to cancel a trip to a conference in London. A few weeks before my departure, however, I seemed to get much better, and the doctor said it would be okay to go ahead with my plans.

Halfway through my flight across the Atlantic Ocean, I noticed that my breathing was becoming more labored. By the time I reached my London hotel, I was in respiratory distress. I'd taken all my medicine, but it didn't seem to be helping much. I thought I'd feel better if I could drink some hot tea and immerse myself in hot water, so I filled the bathtub as high as I could and made sure that my chest was completely submerged.

Although this technique had worked for me in the past, I was still suffering and seemed to be getting worse. I was breathing so shallowly that it felt as if I wasn't getting any air at all. I saw my face in the mirror across from the bathtub, and I noticed that my lips had begun to turn blue. It was at that moment that I realized I could die. I tried to get out of the tub to call for help, but I didn't have enough strength to sit up.

My first thought was that I couldn't let myself die in this foreign land, so far away from my family. But as I struggled unsuccessfully for oxygen, I finally let go, thinking that if it were my destiny to pass on in this place, then that would have to be okay.

As soon as I gave up my resistance, I felt my life force shoot through the top of my head—my crown chakra. I was speeding across a vast black field, heading toward a pinpoint of light in the distance. I remember remarking to myself that it wasn't a dark tunnel as most people reported, but a wide, black expanse. And as I looked around, I saw light beings on either side of me heading in the same direction, speeding to their own pinpoints of light. I remember thinking, *Oh, they must be dying, too.*

It was only a moment before I found myself in a beautiful, light-filled space, standing on a ridge above a glistening river. When I started to take in the scene around me, I noticed that to my left was the same guide who'd taken me to the realm between lifetimes in my dream more than 20 years earlier. We communicated as we had then—not through speech, but through thoughts.

He didn't have to tell me where I was, however. I knew that I was at the passageway between physical life and death. The glistening river lay before us; and on the opposite bank, a group of people were waiting for me. My father was standing next to his mother, along with other family members and friends who'd passed on, including my great-grandparents. There were also beloved pets, as well as other people and animals I didn't recognize. Somehow I knew that they were soul companions from previous lifetimes, coming to greet me again.

As soon as I saw my father standing there, I desperately longed to go to him. Because he had died in a car accident, I never had the chance to say good-bye; and I never really got over his death. Looking at him across that river, I felt our deep connection renewed. I knew that we could communicate through our thoughts, and I told him how much I missed him. He responded that he was always with me. I longed to go to him, and somehow I knew that I could easily step off the ledge and pass over the river to the other side.

I felt so compelled to be with him that I didn't know what to do, and I struggled with the decision for what seemed like a very long time. I kept looking from my father's face to my guide, wondering what I should do. When I again told my father that I wanted to be with him, he assured me that we'd be together very soon. This shocked me and I thought, *Well, if I'm going to die soon, I might as well just pass over now.*

When my father heard that thought, he responded, *If you do go back, it will seem like a long time until we're back together; but trust me, it will just be the blink of an eye in <u>real</u> time.*

Although this confused me, it also soothed me somewhat. I knew it was time to make my decision—and I was free to go either way. I also knew that once I passed over that river, I wouldn't be able to return in my present identity and body.

In my confusion, I turned to the guide standing next to me once more. He looked at me and told me, *You know you have more to do this time around.*

I realized he was right, and I was about to repeat his sentiment: *Yes, I know I have more to do,* but I couldn't get the entire statement out.

As soon as I began to think, *Yes, I know . . . ,* I immediately snapped out of that place and traveled in an instant back to my own body. The energy of my soul returning to my physical form was so rapid that it seemed to slam into my body, causing water to splash out of the bathtub.

I lay there in stunned silence, trying to take in the whole experience. I knew that one decisive moment had directed my destiny back to this plane. I understood that it had been the right thing to do, yet I was sad that I didn't have a chance to say good-bye to my father one last time. I felt his presence with me, however, and I knew I would see him again "soon" in *real* time. I also felt the arms of my grandmother—his mother—around me. She'd suffered from asthma her entire life, and I could feel her bringing me strength and healing.

Slowly—very slowly—I started to breathe more deeply. I don't know how long I stayed there, but by the time I was able to lift myself out of the tub, the water had turned very cold. I staggered to bed and bundled up, and as I gathered the covers around me, I felt the love of many spirits there, too. I fell asleep knowing that a healing was taking place, and I was certain that my life would never be the same.

Time and Truth

Personally experiencing this type of phenomenon can shift intellectual beliefs into heartfelt truths. The revelations that such events bring about then become the filter for all of life. This was the case for me, and I want to share with you what I came to understand as a result of the wonderful gift that terrible illness brought me.

1. Life Goes on After Death

I'd always believed in the continuity of life, but this experience made it absolutely real for me. Some scientists say that the images individuals see in a near-death experience are the result of randomly firing neurons that trigger distant memories. But if this is the case, why are all the "memories" of people who have passed on? Why would my deceased father be "remembered" and not my mother? And why would I have a memory of a friend who passed away long ago, yet not a single recollection that included my twin sister, with whom I've spent most of my life? How could random firings skip the one person with whom I have millions of memories?

From the perspective of someone who's been through it, there's only one explanation that seems reasonable. It's not random neural activity and triggered memories; it's the transportation of the soul to that mystic realm we go to between our earthly existences. Each spirit will arrive there in its own time, connecting with those people who've gone ahead. Such is the continuity of life. Energy doesn't end; it just transforms.

In the energetic realm, we're all light beings. The people seen in a near-death experience show themselves as they were in life so that we can identify them. This is also true when we engage in spirit communication. Souls identify themselves by their looks and the clothes they wore—but of course they have no need for any of these things on "the other side."

2. Death Isn't Predestined

Some people believe that the hour and day of our death is determined before we're born. While that may be the case in some situations, in my experience, I had a very real choice. I knew without a doubt that I could either cross that river and move on to the next cycle of life or go back. It was totally up to me. I wasn't being directed in either way, and the result of that decision was a genuine unknown—both to me and to all of the souls present.

It was clear that my spirit guide and all those on the other side of the river were just waiting to find out what I would decide; and for a few moments, I honestly didn't know myself. I'd been devastated by my father's death just a few years earlier, and the thought of being able to be with him again was truly compelling. Although my spirit guide reminded me that I still had work to do,

I knew beyond a shadow of a doubt that I was free to make whichever decision I desired.

3. We Each Have a Personal Destiny to Fulfill

Our destiny may not lie in specific acts, but our influence is important in the world. When I was trying to make my decision, the comment from my spirit guide about having more work to do resonated deeply in my heart. I had a sense of knowing that I wasn't done with what my soul had planned—and hadn't learned all of the lessons that I came for. Although I didn't know the specifics of what I still had to accomplish, I felt that my soul's intentions were calling me back. I didn't realize it at the time, but the kids that I had yet to adopt were already small children in Russia. The book that I'd written was waiting to be published; and countless experiences, relationships, and adventures were waiting to be had.

In that moment of decision, I felt compelled to return to face my future and engage in all of the lessons that lay ahead. Yes, we all have a destiny waiting to be fulfilled. Whether it's about family, work, or personal evolution, each soul has its plans. It's up to us to muster the courage to face them.

4. Time Is Not as It Seems

I'd been studying the space-time continuum for many years when I had that near-death experience, but studying and living through an event are two vastly different things. Somehow my soul was able to slip from linear Earth time to the eternal present of the spirit realm. In that place, it seemed as though there were no future and no past, just the ever-present now.

My father's comment about being reunited in the blink of an eye created a powerful shift in my way of thinking. I realized that the limitations of time, space, fear, and urgency are merely constraints that we place upon ourselves. The soul sees our journey for what it is—an eternal array of opportunities. The difficulties are as fleeting as the joys, with life expressing itself in every common moment.

At the Crossroads of Now and Then

There's nothing so elusive as time. It exists and is labeled by hours, days, and years; yet it can't be held in any but the most abstract fashion, such as memory or anticipation. Perhaps, as I discussed in Chapter 1, the past and future exist in parallel universes. In the energetic present, a fleeting thought can split into two parallel realities, leading to potentially different outcomes. And this may not be limited to just the future—it's entirely possible that those "multi-verses" carry different pasts and presents as well.

Scientists commonly believe that all time exists simultaneously, and what we perceive as the sequential passage from minute to minute is merely an experiential phenomenon. This concept of the space-time continuum is truly difficult to wrap our mind around: *How can all time exist at the same time? And if that's really the case, what's going on in the future and past as we move through each present moment?*

Some people call the space-time continuum a deep, wide ocean where some currents move in one direction and others—even if they're very close—take an entirely opposite course. I see time as a field of potentiality, with past, present, and future potentials all located on the same plane of existence. The difference between each is a matter of vibration—with past and future happening at different vibratory rates. Our linear movement from hour to hour happens at a much denser resonance, allowing us to live in the sense of "real" time. The past falls away in less dense movement, and the future spans out in front of us, a plane of information waiting to be formed and experienced. In this way, sequential time is linear, moving us through what we see and feel; but the rest of time still exists in vibrating pure potential. This simultaneity of past, present, and future is truly an important concept when dealing with our encoded consciousness. It gives us the opportunity to go back and rewrite the past and move forward to formulate the future.

Déjà Vu

The ability to energetically move through time can have a great impact on your life. It's one of the explanations for the phenomenon known as *déjà vu*, a French term meaning "already seen." You've probably had this kind of experience at some point. You walk into a place you've never been before, but somehow you know what it looks like—and even what's going to happen next. You meet a stranger, but there's a startling sense of familiarity. Or during a conversation, for just a fraction of a second, you know what the other person is going to say next, and you feel as though you've lived this exact moment in time before.

How could such an unusual, brief, yet deeply moving event take place? Many people say that déjà vu is a memory from a past life—and it very well may be. But it can also result from your innate ability to move through time on an energetic level, a surprisingly common experience that very few are conscious of. It's often called *astral* or *mental projection* and usually occurs in periods of quiet or when you're sleeping. The etheric body—*the part of you that's core energy and consciousness*—can move through the multidimensional Universe of time and space. Often when you sleep, your astral energy will go visiting, which is why past-life memories can come so easily in dreams. It's also why you feel so very familiar with the déjà vu event.

During the night, when your astral body goes forward in time, you experience a glimpse into some future potential. It soon returns to the physical body; and when you awaken, you may remember a dream, or the event may simply recede into your subconscious. You continue to travel through life in linear time and eventually come upon the very moment you visited. That sense of familiarity flashes through your mind, a spark of knowing that's both surprising and strangely reassuring.

I've had several such experiences. In one remarkable instance, I woke up from a dream that was so unusual that I immediately described it to my husband at the time. I'd dreamed that I was in a foreign city where all the buildings seemed to be white. I was in a taxi with a blonde woman whom I didn't know, and she was interpreting what the driver was saying about the neighborhood. It was just a short vignette, but it felt amazingly familiar—so much so that I just couldn't believe I'd dream about someone I didn't know in a city I hadn't been to, yet have it feel so real.

Two years later, I'd made plans to meet my husband's sister, who worked as a nanny in Paris. We were taking a taxi somewhere, and I noticed that all the buildings were white. When she started interpreting something the driver was saying, that dream came back to me in a flash. But it wasn't just a dream—it was déjà vu. I *had* traveled there. This was real life, yet everything was exactly as it had been in that distant vision. The place, the people, the experience—all of it sparked some sort of epiphany. It was so profoundly real that I felt as if the Universe were giving me a glimpse into the truth about the space-time continuum and our ability to move freely through it.

Fate or Potential?

The realization that all time exists at the same time brings up the question of predestination. If the future is taking place right now, does that mean those events are already set?

In spite of that very specific déjà vu experience, I believe the answer is *no*. Although I've had many similar sensations of familiarity, that particular one was a revelation because of my conscious memory of the dream. In that sleeping state, my energetic body went forward at least two years and experienced this interesting event. I remembered having been there; and over time, my life led me back in that direction.

But does this mean that everything is scripted in advance? I believe that our soul plans lessons for us—not necessarily events. The Heisenberg uncertainty principle reveals that the world exists in a state of pure potential, a constant state of flow and flux. This is the case in the physical world of waves and particles, and it's also true in our eternal lives. The soul brings its lessons into this existence, and events are formed that help facilitate our growth. The sooner we learn, the sooner we can transform what we're experiencing. Thus, the future exists in an energetic potential that can be changed. And although it may sound strange, the past exists in a resonant memory that can be revisited and altered as well.

Your *immutable karma* was determined before birth. These are the things planned out by your soul and others, including who your parents are, where you're born, and what gender and race you'll be. As its name indicates, immutable karma doesn't change and is part of your consciousness code for this life.

Your *mutable karma,* however, refers to those elements that can be modified as you grow. This is within your power. If you ignore your lessons, you'll bring them back over and over again, but your future is *not* set in stone. If you grasp your opportunities, destiny is yours to create. Likewise, the past and its effects can be mutable, too. But before you can rewrite history and change its influence, you have to find out what happened.

Passports to the Past

There are many ways to visit eternity. You can even gather past-life information by looking at the details of your present life.

As you'll discover in Part II of this book, a *conscious investigation* of current issues and circumstances can reveal a lot.

As you explore, remember that this is a journey of the spirit. If you want to open the door to the timeless realm, make sure you meditate on a regular basis. This is important because it sets the energetic stage, calming your body and your brain frequency, increasing your receptivity to the mystic information out there. When your brain frequency is in the *alpha-wave* state (from 8 to 13 cycles per second), you're more relaxed, intuitive, and inspired. This is the vibrational portal through which the information from the Akashic Record comes, so keep a meditation journal and jot down any impressions that may indicate past-life information.

The Akashic Record—also called the Alaya (unending or "store-house") consciousness—is a vast field of information that contains all of the technical, scientific, and creative knowledge throughout time. This is both global and personal in nature. Not only can you become brilliantly inspired by tapping into this force, you can also connect with your own past lives very specifically.

The details of the past are encoded within and are accessible to you. Spending time in the alpha level of brain frequency makes it easier to connect with that information, and the door can open much more easily. Following are some of the most common ways in which you can retrieve long-hidden elements that may still be influencing you today.

Regression

This hypnotic process takes you back to the experiences of specific past lives. You can do a regression with the help of a hypnotist, or you can listen to a guided meditation like the one on the CD inside this book. (It's more thoroughly explained in Chapter 11, so make sure to read that chapter before listening.)

In addition, the CD has a *rescripting* technique that's also described in detail in Chapter 11. I mention it here because when we're talking about the nature of time and our ability to move through it, we must recognize that we have power in the present to actually reformulate the past. We can create a script that changes our karmic code, supplying different emotions and results, as well as far healthier conclusions. Through rescripting, we have the power to heal the patterns we desire to change—even if they originated long ago.

Triggered Associations

These memories surface when you're engaged in an activity that's similar to a particular past-life event. I had just such an experience following a recent surgery. I was trying to roll over in bed, which was difficult because of my abdominal incision. All of a sudden, my bedroom wall turned stark white, as though I were in an old-fashioned hospital. I realized that in a past life I'd just had a stillborn baby. I was overcome with grief, but it made a lot of sense when applied to the present surgery and many other issues in my life.

These episodes come unbidden, often when you're tired, bored, or distracted. But unless you're aware of the potential connection, you might think you're daydreaming and not even realize when a triggered association has taken place.

Spontaneous Memories

Similar to triggered associations, these flashes appear without expectation. However, they often have nothing to do with present circumstances or feelings. Instead, they represent random events floating up from the depths of past-life consciousness. This type of memory can seem even more like daydreaming because it's so foreign and unrelated to anything currently going on. In fact, this information often comes up when you're falling asleep or waking up.

Children have a remarkable number of spontaneous memories that seem to appear out of nowhere. This is likely due to the fact that when we're young, we spend most of our time in the alpha-wave brain frequency. Between the ages of five and seven, however, we start to move up into the higher, more agitated beta state, which is above 13 cycles per second, so conscious past-life memories slowly decrease.

Many children I know have relayed their spontaneous memories to me. When my nephew was four years old, my sister and I were in the car with him when he suddenly blurted out, "Remember when I was big, and we lived above the chocolate shop next to the place where they bury people?"

We immediately knew he was having a past-life memory, so we asked him to tell us more. He told us that he worked in a coat factory, going into great detail about the garment he made, describing it as brown with weird pockets and sleeves. He said it was called the American Coat. Years later, my sister and I were in an antique shop and found a catalog from the turn of the century. In it was an item called "The American Coat," which had suede patch pockets and suede patches on the elbows. It only came in brown.

If the children in your life start talking about memories that are strange to you, encourage them, and write down what they tell you, because all too soon this information will be forgotten.

Dreams

Because dreams also occur in the alpha-wave frequency, they can carry a lot of past-life information. So if you have a dream where you're a king or a queen, don't dismiss it! I always recommend keeping a journal by the bed. Whether you're receiving specific past-life scenarios, or just getting important information from metaphorical dreams, it's always helpful to record your impressions and review them in light of what's going on in your life.

Past-Life Readings

There are many psychics, mediums, and intuitives who give past-life readings. This may be because the door to the energetic realm is open so frequently for them, and their access to the Akashic Record is undeterred. When they connect with a client, they pick up the resonance of that person's unique signature vibration, creating an automatic link to the client's particular information.

Although I didn't realize what was happening, I started receiving this type of information in my counseling days. I'd get glimpses—sometimes just a flash, and sometimes a whole moving picture that played out in my mind—revealing important information about the person I was working with.

I occasionally asked, "Has this ever happened to you?" Then I described what I'd seen. Sometimes my client was surprised and recalled what I told them from long ago in this life; sometimes it wasn't familiar at all. Over time, however, I realized that I was often being given past-life details, specific material relating to the issue we were dealing with at that time.

Your history isn't limited to the events of this life. Your inherent identity is woven into a vast tapestry of information, and all the details of who you are and what you've been through can be revealed to you. You *do* have the ability to visit eternity because you already live there—past and future, here and now. When you discover your unknown past, you can not only change what's going on in the present, you can open yourself to your soul's intention. And when you align with *that* purpose, you'll find out that every moment is filled with infinite possibilities.

Chapter 3

KARMA AND YOUR ENCODED CONSCIOUSNESS

In the vast ocean of time, your eternal soul is moving from one current to another, maintaining its intrinsic spiritual identity all the way. This is your soul's consciousness—a field of information devoted to you, spanning from the beginning of time to the present moment and beyond.

Your eternal consciousness has been encoded with data and emotional energy from lifetime to lifetime—and it's influencing you right now. The fact is that you're carrying vibrations, conclusions, and even emotions from the long-forgotten past. These memories—both from this existence and previous ones—can be held in your physical cells and your life force, contributing to the resonant signature that's yours and yours alone. From your first incarnation to this very moment, your history has been recorded, helping to shape the person you are now, as well as the destiny you'll create.

Evolution of the Soul

The ongoing process of reincarnation and encoded consciousness is an elegant system of energetic exchange and information storage. The emotional context and the conclusions that become encrypted are based on the myriad experiences that each lifetime brings.

Each soul's evolutionary path has a purpose, including the lessons we're meant to learn in order to evolve and move forward. Throughout time, our consciousness becomes more complex, layering different experiences and allowing us to develop a deeper awareness of our purpose and underlying truth. When we learn, we free ourselves from old, unhealthy patterns. When we don't, we merely accumulate more and more of the energy we're meant to change.

For example, if you've had past lives as an alcoholic, the sensations and longings that accompany those experiences become part of your karma code, compelling you to lean in that direction yet again. It may be your purpose to release the addiction this time around. If you succeed, it not only breaks the pattern, it shatters the code and allows your soul to evolve into a higher vibration of existence. On the other hand, if the tendency toward alcoholism is repeated, then that drive will become more deeply encoded, making it even more emotional and difficult to heal the next time around.

Your Own Secret Code

You have your own unique karma code, a driving force in your present life. While most emotional experiences become encoded, many are of little consequence in the scheme of your eternal being. There are some factors, however, that can pretty much guarantee that something will have to be dealt with in subsequent lifetimes. Let's look at the strongest influences on what's likely to be indoctrinated into the deeper energies of your soul's identity.

1. High Emotional Charge and Intensity

Throughout my years as a counselor in private psychological practice, I've often told my clients that the more highly emotionally charged an experience is, the more likely it is to influence them throughout their lives. This is also true in terms of karma. The greater the emotional intensity was back then—whether positive or negative—the greater the impact now. If an event from a past life was extremely pleasurable, such as love or passion, it's pretty much guaranteed to mold this life. Likewise, any severely negative experience such as divorce, financial ruin, illness, loss, or betrayal will leave an emotional imprint—but the influence doesn't stop there.

The *energy* of those experiences and your responding *conclusions* are encoded. For example, if you were betrayed by a husband in a past life, the conclusion that men can't be trusted may be deeply encoded in this life. As a result, you could be unconsciously resisting romantic relationships, all the while you're desperately longing for one. This sends out conflicting intentions where your goals are concerned, creating obstacles that you may not even be aware of.

It's equally true that the highly charged events of *this* life are planting the seeds of future experiences. For this reason, it's extremely important that you ventilate the emotional energy of your difficult experiences, and then go on to reframe any toxic conclusions you've made.

Although present problems may have their seeds in previous existences, the evolution of your eternal life requires you to deal with the here-and-now. No matter when they happen, your highly charged experiences need to be addressed. Your life will keep raising the issue until you deal with all the emotional, cognitive, and even physiological ramifications.

2. Physical Problems and Brutal Memories

Some of the most deeply encoded memories from past lives come from violence and extreme physical disruption. In fact, it's not uncommon for our present maladies to be sourced in the bodily traumas of previous incarnations. For example, nearly drowning in a past life could be connected to current respiratory problems. It could also be a valid explanation for a phobia of water.

Violent injuries and trauma are so emotionally charged that they can be extremely influential in subsequent lifetimes. Surgeries are often located in the same area of the body where past-life injuries have taken place. I've seen this a lot in my readings and regressions, such as the one that occurred during a recent seminar I was giving.

Upon returning to the lecture hall after the lunch break, a woman came up to me and said, "Can you give me a quick past-life reading?"

Although I was running late and didn't intend to, a powerful and vivid image stopped me cold. I saw her fighting in a battle, with a sword coming down into her chest.

I told her, "In a past life, you were stabbed in the chest by a sword," and I indicated exactly where the blade cut down and across her chest.

The woman gasped and exclaimed, "I just had surgery there for breast cancer!"

I felt that her lesson was self-love and self-priority. She wasn't supposed to be in battle then, and she's not supposed to be fighting other people's battles now.

This isn't an uncommon scenario. Physical abuse, attacks, and even accidental injuries can carry strong energetic vibrations. Experiences are encoded deeply in our consciousness and are brought forward into cellular memory. I'm not saying that every single physical problem has a past-life source, but there are often threads that tie our more serious or chronic conditions to highly charged issues from the past.

3. An Untimely, Unexpected, or Violent Death

A major influence on your karma code is the type and timing of your death in previous lives. If it happened at an early age or was abrupt and unexpected, it can cause a significant disruption to the soul's path and intended lessons, compelling the spirit to return right away. An interesting example of this can be seen in the data of today's population.

The largest demographic in the U.S. is the group called the *baby boomers.* This phenomenon isn't limited to the United States, however. All over the world, there's a significant population that was born between 1946 and 1964.

People think this is the result of the peace and prosperity following World War II. Although that may be partially true, there was also a karmic influence on the increase in population.

During the war, millions upon millions of lives were cut short in abrupt and violent ways. When this happens, there's a monumental amount of unfinished business—both for the individuals and the groups involved—and the souls are often not ready or willing to leave their earthly experience. The result was a quick return in the years directly following the war!

Death is an emotional experience at any age, but when life is unexpectedly ripped away, the soul feels compelled to rejoin the adventure. It not only wants to experience the myriad pleasures of life, it also longs to finish the lessons encoded in its deepest spiritual intentions.

Youth itself has a high emotional charge. People are making plans and falling in love, filled with enthusiasm and expectation for what's to come. When that excitement is cut short, it's natural for the soul to want to jump right back in. Death in old age, however, is less emotionally charged. The spirit has experienced a lot and may on some level even yearn for a clearer connection with its source. In these cases, there may be a far greater readiness to move on, and a less rapid return in terms of earthly time.

Shared Karma

We may come back right away or choose to wait awhile and return with our core group of souls. We share karma the way we share consciousness, so based on our common experiences, we return with lessons that link us together. Sometimes the shared karma is limited to small groups such as family, friends, or co-workers; sometimes it expands to entire cultures and countries.

Having a sick child could be shared karma for a young couple, and their lessons must be approached both individually and to-gether. A larger group sharing karma could be colleagues learning that their company is closing. And much more expansive exam-ples can be found when war, famine, or natural disasters devastate entire communities or countries.

Such experiences have global lessons for everyone involved, as well as very personal opportunities for each individual. It's up to us to look at our wider experiences to find out what our shared lessons may be. Recent economic patterns could be telling us that we should shift our priorities, let go of old materialistic obsessions, and find greater gratification in our relationships and personal pursuits.

When you're dealing with an incident of shared karma, it's often helpful to discuss the experience with the other people involved. Investigate what the lessons and opportunities may be, and see if you can help each other arrive at a deeper understanding of what it all means. Your shared intention to heal past influences can accelerate the process for yourself and everyone else.

I recently had an interesting shared karma encounter during a seminar I was conducting in Lily Dale, New York. After participating in a meditation, an audience member said he'd experienced a past life where he was relocating to that part of New York, trying to start over after the Civil War. After he announced this, other attendees said they'd had similar experiences, discovering past lives at that time with the same emotions of loss and redirection. It turned out that more than half of the class had shared that postwar existence, although most of them didn't know each other in this life. We realized that we were all brought together to put those emotions of loss to rest and to find a deeper spiritual meaning in this time and place.

I find that increased interest in all things spiritual is another example of shared karma today. There are many people whose pursuit of the sacred was thwarted in past lives, and many who were even persecuted for what they practiced and believed. Countless numbers have been born into this era in order to rectify that old toxic energy and engage in a common intention for spiritual growth as individuals, and for the world at large.

The Eternal You

No matter whom you share your past or present experiences with, you always carry your own unique karma code—the information that's built on the past and influences the future.

All of these things become part of your energetic makeup—an encoded message about who you are now and why you're here this time around. Throughout the book we'll continue exploring what these patterns look like and what they may mean for you right now. This is your karma code, a driving force for your soul's evolution. It's part of the wonderful process of life after life, a vehicle that brings about enlightenment and profound understanding.

Getting Clear about Karma

A very common misconception about karma is that it's a predetermined punishment handed down from some vague but powerful judge. This is not the case. Karma isn't punitive, and it isn't binding! It's the soul's own design—together with other spirits involved. Let's take a look at some of the other misconceptions and find out what karma really is—and what it is *not*.

- *Karma is not:* Punishment or payback for former "misdeeds." Not everything difficult that happens to you comes from a past-life source.

- *Karma IS:* An exchange, return, or understanding of energy patterns and their meanings. Some lessons your soul chooses aren't karmic, but are intentions for expansion.

- *Karma is not:* Predetermined, predestined fate. Lessons are planned, but most technicalities aren't.

- *Karma IS:* Changing, flexible, and mutable. As your consciousness shifts, so does your karma.

- *Karma is not:* Episodic and specific. You don't have to experience every single thing you've put out in past lives.

- *Karma IS:* Issue related. As you heal the pattern and learn the lesson, all related karma is released—even from this and other lifetimes.

Like your DNA, which is a code for your physical makeup and biological identity, your karma code reveals specific information about who you are, what you've been through, and how you've responded to it all. The eternal consciousness of your soul records the things that make you . . . you. This code includes:

1. *Hidden memories of past events*

2. *Emotional responses to those events, including feelings such as fear, rejection, joy, and excitement*

3. *Important conclusions based on those emotions, especially with respect to your value, worthiness, safety, and power—as well as the power of others*

4. *Physical issues and the conclusions built around them*

5. *Intentions for lessons and personal growth, including connection with, and expression of, your spiritual truth*

> *Karma has two main purposes:*
>
> 1. *To allow us to experience and understand the energies we may have perpetuated in past experiences*
>
> 2. *To help us learn important lessons that may have eluded us in previous existences—lessons that are not only important for our own loving enlightenment, but also for the expansion of love in the Universe*

These two purposes come together when we realize that it's the learning of the lesson that ameliorates the return of old energies. For example, if you were a murderer in a past incarnation, that doesn't necessarily mean you have to be murdered now in order to release the encoded karma. All you have to do is realize the intrinsic value of life and learn to have genuine reverence for the lives of others. This will shift your consciousness and break the old code, allowing you to reformulate a new and higher intention and project a more resonant and harmonic vibration.

Of course, if you're resistant to the lesson, it's entirely possible that someone you love could be murdered in order to force you to realize how truly valuable life is. This would be a return of energy, causing a powerful epiphany in your understanding. But it would be your *realization,* not the event itself, which would complete the lesson. Having to experience this may sound extreme, but from the soul's point of view, it actually isn't that dramatic at all.

Your Spirit's Point of View

People often ask me, "Why would we keep putting ourselves through this?" After all, life can be difficult—sometimes unbearably so.

But the soul has a longer, grander view of things. It doesn't just see trouble, even if that's a large part of what's happening this time around. No, the soul notices all of life's finer nuances. It revels in the joy of every sunset and each sweet-smelling flower, in every baby's laugh and sip of wine. All of these things—every wonderful moment—can be very enticing motivations to face the fullness of life. But the soul sees something even greater and more compelling than the simple pleasures. It's drawn by the powerful opportunities offered even in difficult times—by the courage that results from facing illness, the compassion awakened by assisting others, and the freedom that comes from turning to the Light in the darkest moments.

The soul sees earthly life in a very different way from the personal self. It's similar to an actor who knows he's going to play a role—it may be temporary, but it's important. He knows that the production will end and he'll move on to the next one. If the character he plays is suffering, the actor isn't necessarily bothered by it. In fact, he may think that an extremely difficult and emotional role is a great way to hone his craft—to dig deeper into himself and rise to the challenge of the part.

The soul has much the same attitude. It knows that in real time, the experience on this Earth plane is short—even if it spans 80 or more years as we measure time. And although this role is temporary and quick in terms of eternal reality, the way it's approached is immensely important in terms of evolution. In time the soul will go on to another role, but it's willing to take on difficulty now for the sake of its craft—the craft of enlightenment and love.

Such challenges as illness and poverty are no bigger problems to the eternal self than they are to an actor playing those parts. The soul sees them as important and valuable opportunities to work on its evolution—to achieve goals such as self-mastery; the growth of wisdom, discipline, and expression; and the expansion of love, service, and compassion—in short, the enlightenment that comes from awakening to the spirit within.

How does your soul view the events of your life? It knows that there will be both good and bad, but there's a greater design to the process. You may not have any conscious recollection of your higher plan. Ego, attachments, and desperate desires can get in the way.

But all of that changes when you start to look at things from the soul's point of view. In every experience there's a lesson—a deeper meaning—and it's what you learn that's important, rather than the event itself. Your soul knows that it's not what happens to you, but how you handle it that matters.

Your karma code is driven by your spirit's point of view, and its priorities are important directives that must be addressed. They include:

- Finding the meaning and purpose of your own life

- Asking how you can bring light to the darkness and love to the difficulties

- Opening your heart to the Divine Consciousness within

Prioritizing these eternal perspectives will change the code that brought you here, revealing a new path and redirecting your destiny.

When you take a step back and look at your life, it begins to resemble an amazing jigsaw puzzle. The pieces fit together in very specific ways, although you may not be able to figure out how they all connect. When you add the pieces from past lives, however, you get a much clearer understanding. In time you'll see a panoramic picture of who you've been and what you're meant to do and be this time around. The beauty, purpose, and power of your spirit is a central part of this intriguing scenario, and all of the pieces of your own mystical and eternal puzzle will fall into place when you open your heart to your soul's point of view.

". . . in the superhologram of the universe, past, present, and future are all enfolded and exist simultaneously. This suggests that it might even be possible to some day reach into the superhologram and retrieve from oblivion the long-forgotten past."

— MICHAEL TALBOT, *BEYOND THE QUANTUM*

PART II

Cracking Your Karma
CODE

Chapter 4

THE BODY ELECTRIC

Your soul is eternal. There is a beginning and an end to your body's *physical* existence, but your spirit never dies. It moves through time without limitation.

With each life you have a new earthly body, but that's not the extent of your personal makeup. You also have an energetic body, an essence of light and vibration that takes the form of each new incarnation, filling it up with spiritual energy and resonating outward from its physical location with the brilliance of your eternal self.

This has many names. It's sometimes called the *astral* or *etheric* body, and it's also known as the *aura*. Although there are slight differences in the definitions of each of these terms, the important thing to remember here is that you do indeed have an energetic form. At the core is your spiritual identity, which has been with you in each and every incarnation.

Much of the encoded information from previous physical experiences gets stored here. As you go through life after life, the traumas, illnesses, and injuries leave an imprint on your energetic body. For example, if you were stabbed in the back in a past existence, the vibrations of that experience are likely to be held in the same place in your energetic body in this life. Just as a broken ankle in childhood could manifest in adulthood as arthritis in the same joint, the scars and traumas from previous lives can be held in vibrational storage, and surface as physical issues much later.

The energetic memory of some incidents may be fleeting and not have much influence. Yet other, more serious events from previous incarnations may create a significant effect on your body. The more chronic, difficult, or pervasive a present condition is, the more important it is to acknowledge the possibility that it could originate in the past. For this reason, the information gleaned from past-life investigations can go a long way toward healing not only energetic memories, but also their physical manifestations in the present.

A Lung Full of Guilt

I learned about the physical component of encoded information personally when I had my very first past-life regression. I was about 22 years old, and I was amazed by what I found out!

My life has been peppered with allergies and infections, which increased in severity as I got older. Once, while taking a class in past-life interpretation, I asked the instructor what my chronic sinus problems could indicate about my previous experience. She responded, "You must have been very *snotty* in a past life."

Although her comment made me laugh, I knew there must be a karmic component to these recurring physical issues. I wasn't compelled to dig any further, however, until my sinus infections expanded into bronchial distress.

When I was about 19 or 20, I started suffering from chronic asthma and lung infections. This was very distressing and even became debilitating at times. After a couple years of taking antibiotics, steroids, and respiratory medications, I decided to take a deeper look at the past-life potential for my condition. I was 22 by that point, and I'd spent the preceding five years studying all sorts of Eastern philosophies and religions. I'd never had a past-life regression, however, and I was wary. I knew that I was going to be hypnotized, and I had the same questions that most people have about that process:

- What if I couldn't be hypnotized?

- What if I was unable to get any information—
  or if it was embarrassing?

- How is it even possible to talk about my experience,
  yet stay relaxed enough to continue the hypnosis?

- What if my discoveries were traumatic or upsetting—
  could that make my physical condition worse?

- What if reincarnation didn't really exist and I was
  just being a fool in pursuing this?

All of these questions were swimming in my mind as I anxiously drove to my session. I expressed some of my fears to the man conducting the hypnosis, and he reassured me. He told me that it wasn't unusual to have misgivings before hypnosis, whether it was a regression or not, and that the misgivings only increase when the subject is something so abstract and unfamiliar as a past life.

He made it clear that no matter what information I received, I'd be able to express it without coming out of the hypnotic state, and I'd remember everything. In fact, in the days following the regression, it would all become clearer and clearer, and other memories would spontaneously come to the surface because the door had been opened. He also reassured me that if I were unable to relax or access any information at all, we could try again at a later date.

Before our session, the therapist asked me to set the stage. He wanted to know specifically what kind of information I was seeking and what issue I was working on. I described my history of sinus infections and, more recently, chronic lung infections and asthma. I also told him that I was in the habit—almost nightly for the past two years—of waking up at precisely 4:15 A.M., wheezing and unable to breathe. It was disruptive because I never got a good night's sleep, and I had to sit up and take my medicine until my breathing became regular again. In my mind, the reason was chemical. I thought that the asthma medicine I took just before bed was merely wearing off at that moment, causing my breathing to be more constrained.

So we created the specific intention to find out about the past life (or lives) that contributed to my present respiratory problems. After a relaxing induction, I found myself immersed in a scene where I was the main character, and somehow I knew precisely what was going on. I knew that I was living in England, in charge of five young children as the governess for a wealthy family. I'd regressed into that life just a few minutes before the seeds of my present asthma were planted. . . .

I was woken up by the sounds of a little boy crying. He was calling out my name—Emma in that life. I looked at the clock on the mantel over the fireplace. It was 4:15. I stood up and reached for the candle by my bedside, going over to the hearth where I lit it from the fire.

I started walking in the direction of the crying child, knowing where I was and where I was going. I remember the cold marble under my bare feet and the long white nightgown brushing against my ankles. I also recall walking by a mirror. Although I didn't stop, I saw in my peripheral vision that I had long black hair, and I appeared to be about 19 or 20—which was when my asthma problem started in this life.

I went into the nursery where a beautiful little blond boy was crying, coughing, and having difficulty breathing. He was obviously suffering from what my present self knew to be pneumonia. I could hear the rasping in his chest, and I was distressed to think that he might not live. I set the candle down on the bedside table next to a little metal soldier dressed in the red cloak of a British military uniform.

It was interesting because my present self was registering all this information, yet my past self was desperate and emotionally involved. I knew this little boy was sick, and I knew that somehow it was my responsibility. I chastised myself for letting the children go out in the rain, for it was after that event that the boy became ill.

As he was saying my name and having a more and more difficult time breathing, I took him in my arms and began to pray, saying, "Please, God, make him better. Please don't take him. *Give this to me,* but don't take him!" As I was trying to bargain with God and asking to take on the illness, the beloved little boy who'd been my charge died in my arms.

The connection was clear. I felt horrible guilt and responsibility for the death of this child. I encoded those feelings, along with the desire to punish myself for his death. The request to have the illness myself had become a driving force in my present life and was hanging on in my cellular memory. I knew that I'd have to do a lot of work in order to release the emotions, conclusions, and physical issues that went along with that event.

After that regression, I never again woke up wheezing at 4:15 A.M. Sometimes all you need is information in order to clear an emotional charge, as well as the effects that go along with it. Sometimes, however, you need to do more work.

It has taken me a long time to break the chain of asthma and lung infections; and although I can go years without an episode, I still have some problems now and then. A recent flare-up made me aware of some other incarnations tied to this ongoing condition, and responsibility continues to be a theme.

There are times when past-life information can reveal something that will make us feel guilty, faulty, or responsible in some way. After all, each existence is a part of our eternal process, and our shared intentions move us through many different types of experiences—good and bad. But faulting ourselves for past-life mistakes won't heal the present. What we need to remember is that we did the best we could—given the information, history, environment, and energy of that life.

It became incumbent upon me to let go of the encoded blame for that boy's death, and to release the sense of responsibility that I'd projected into many other areas. Guilt, responsibility, and caretaking have been issues throughout my present life. I hadn't realized it, but I'd taken the intention of being in charge of that boy and globalized it, creating a lifestyle where I felt responsible for pretty much everyone.

When I became a psychotherapist, I was on call 24/7. I took the profession very seriously, to the point of putting my personal life second to my clients' needs. In my constant longing to take care of others, I lost myself. It turned out that whenever I refused to set boundaries or prioritize my own life, I got another lung infection. It became clear that I hadn't released that guilt and responsibility issue yet. I had to doggedly restructure my approach to life. I had to find out that it was okay to make myself a priority—I could be loving to other people and to myself at the same time.

When I was able to set boundaries and take care of myself along with taking care of others, the lung infections and asthma slowly started to decrease. Whenever I brought balance to my life, I brought harmony and health to my breathing. Even now, when respiratory stuff resurfaces, it's a reminder that I'm worthy of my own priority and self-care.

Issues do return—and so do people. The boy in that past-life regression was to appear in this life in a very important way. I had another lesson yet to learn from him, which I'll discuss later. Until then, keep this in mind: *Not every karmic relationship is one you must take on.*

Physical Signals of Past-Life Experiences

There are many past-life signs all around you, ones that you can discern just by looking at your patterns and your life. Throughout this and the following chapters, there will be questions that you can explore in your journal. The answers may come spontaneously, or they may need some thought and introspection. It can be helpful to do the following meditation, which is a body dialogue—a quiet discussion with the part of yourself where the symptoms or condition may reside. Relax your mind and open your heart to hearing the answers you receive from within.

Body Dialogue Meditation

Get into a comfortable position and take a few deep, cleansing breaths. Let go of all thoughts, concerns, and expectations.

Consider the part of the body or the condition you want to get information about. Let your consciousness slowly go there with peaceful, open intentions. Rest your awareness there for a few moments, and then ask your body these questions:

1. What is the meaning or lesson this is meant to bring me?

Be still and wait to see what the answer may be. You may receive only a word or a phrase, but let yourself note what it is.

2. Is there a past-life connection to what's going on now?

Let yourself pause and relax further. You may see an image, hear some words, or even just have a sense of something. Even if you don't understand it all now, it will become clearer to you over time.

Let yourself take note of whatever arrives. Even if nothing comes at first, try the dialogue again at a later time. You may find yourself receiving information in your dreams or peaceful moments as you go through your day. Trust what you get, and write it down.

It's extremely helpful to investigate the signals that are already apparent in your everyday life. This conscious consideration can be instrumental in two important ways:

1. It can reveal specific details about past and present issues.

2. It stimulates the unconscious memory of deeply encoded information, increasing the potential for a profound awakening, which can lead to a dynamic consciousness shift.

So let's take a look at what some of your present physical experiences could be telling you about past-life events. Remember, not every symptom or incident is linked to a past event, but there's always a message for you—perhaps a lesson to learn, an opportunity to clear old emotions, or a reminder to change unhealthy conclusions or habits. Your body holds many metaphors for you, and discomfort or imbalance is always something that you should check out.

As you go through the following potential karmic clues, jot down any connection that comes to mind. You may instantly come up with an interpretation of a physical issue and its meaning in your life. Trust your intuition and record any possible interpretation you get. If the significance doesn't come to you right away, let yourself meditate on it. Open your heart and mind to the potential meaning these experiences are bringing. As you compile the information from this chapter and those that follow, you'll begin to see a *karmic profile* developing. This not only opens the door to your intuitive investigations, it helps clear the karma and bring greater harmony and balance to both your present process and your soul's evolution.

Chronic Conditions

If you suffer from a chronic condition such as arthritis, asthma, high blood pressure, gastrointestinal issues, recurring migraines, or other persistent problems, it's very likely that these originated in a past life or perhaps even several past lives. This is especially true in cases where you've suffered from the condition for most of your current life. It's possible that you've had this before, or that you've suffered repeated traumas to the area involved.

Your etheric body holds unhealed memories and brings their vibrations to the same location in your physical form from life to life. For example, if you had a head injury in a past existence, it could result in chronic migraines now. It would be important, then, to investigate the emotions and conclusions of that previous experience so that they can be released and reversed. Understanding and turning around both past and present energetic issues will clear them from your karma code and bring healing to today's condition.

At a recent seminar, a woman complained about persistent and severe acid reflux. As she was talking about her condition, a past-life episode unfolded before my eyes. She'd been a slave brought to America from Africa on one of the horrible ships where people were chained together and forced to spend days on end in a shoulder-to-shoulder reclining position. In that experience, she was fed very little, and what she did receive was practically inedible. Between the rolling ship and the bug-infested food, she couldn't keep anything down. The misery, resentment, and sense of powerlessness became encoded in her energetic memories and her eternal consciousness.

Upon further investigation, we found that her mother in this life had been her captor in that one, and the vibration of the present relationship reflected her lack of freedom and power. Her soul longed for her to rid herself of the old energies and conclusions—and to redefine herself according to her eternal value and unlimited power. Not only did she need to release the hold her past had on her spirit and body, but she also had to make her timeless truth a reality in her present relationship with her mother. She knew that she needed to set boundaries and reclaim her power, making it clear to her mother that she was taking back control.

This is an important lesson: whenever we initiate a healing of past-life problems, we must support it with our current choices, behavior, and beliefs!

Take a moment to jot down the physical conditions you've had to deal with in this life. Do they bring to mind any potential past-life connections? What do you think is the message or lesson they may hold for you? And what personal changes can you make to support the lesson and your soul's intention for mastery and growth?

Allergies, Asthma, and Other Respiratory Problems

There are many reasons why people develop allergies and breathing difficulties—sourced in both this and previous incarnations. Severe allergies—those that can cause anaphylaxis and death—can very likely be traced back to extremely traumatic past-life experiences. Chronic but not life-threatening allergies such as skin rashes can indicate past resentments. I had a client who was allergic to most metals and couldn't wear jewelry next to her skin. Silver caused an especially itchy, bumpy rash. When we did a regression, we found that she'd labored in the silver mines of Colorado. She'd also experienced some discomfort in small, closed spaces in her current life. While it didn't impair her functioning, it had been a noticeably chronic issue, and she was amazed to find out that the two problems were connected.

Allergies can also indicate occupations or locations of past lives. For instance, I once had a client who developed celiac disease, a severe allergy to gluten, which is most notably found in wheat. We discovered that she'd been a wheat farmer in Oklahoma at the time of the dust bowl. Although she'd worked hard to save her farm, she lost everything, including a child who had died in infancy. We found that the emotionally charged, encoded information from this one trauma had not only led to her celiac disease, but it had also resulted in a deep fear of financial loss and a severely overprotective relationship with her present-life children.

Breathing problems could indicate a past life in which you were suffocated. It might be a literal suffocation or a metaphorical one, where you weren't allowed to be yourself, honor your needs, or express your feelings. Throat problems—whether related to allergies, infections, or other reasons such as cancer—can indicate a literal strangulation or a symbolic one, where you weren't allowed to speak your truth. If you're having throat or lung problems today, please consider that this may be a karmic directive for you: *Make sure you honor your spirit's intention to speak and honor your truth in every relationship and area of your life.*

Breathing problems, of course, can also be caused by current activities such as smoking, but the compulsion to engage in such addictive activities could come from past-life codes as well. It's important not to get too caught up in the details of past or present sources. If something is a significant issue for you, look for the lesson. That's the key to cracking your karma code.

Do you have any allergies? If so, how and when do they manifest, and what do you think they represent? Could specific occupations or locations be involved? What about skin or respiratory conditions?

Have a dialogue with your body and see what issues may need to be addressed regarding any chronic physical issues.

Breaks, Injuries, and Surgeries

Whenever there's an invasive trauma, it's very likely that this part of the body has been injured before. I once had a client who was in a car accident as a young man in which he broke both of his legs. They were so severely damaged that he had to have a number of surgeries to insert pins and reconnect the bones. While he was coming out of anesthesia, he had vivid dreams of a life where he'd been a mason, constructing a church. The wall he'd been working on collapsed on top of him, crushing both his legs and leaving him unable to walk. For the rest of that life, he had to live with his mother—never marrying, and never recovering from his anger and frustration.

The present-life car accident, although traumatic, was a less severe version of this event. Luckily, modern medicine was able to literally set things straight. However, this past-life revelation uncovered some very important current issues for him. It revealed why he felt so dependent upon his mother, and why he was still (at the age of 28) afraid to set out on his own. After recovering from his final surgery, he was able to move on, literally and figuratively. As painful as the accident and the following surgeries were, he eventually saw them as a blessing, a catalyst to releasing a deeply encoded pattern. Until he was free of it, he hadn't realized how pervasive his fear and isolation had become.

Have you had any surgeries or injuries indicating that an old trauma is still holding a lesson for you? Consider what past event may have triggered this present experience. Dialogue with that area of the body, and ask yourself what you can do to let go of the old emotions and create new conclusions. Scars and birthmarks can also indicate past traumatic events. Take some time to investigate what present meaning they may be bringing you.

Serious or Fatal Illnesses

Critical or catastrophic illnesses—whether they happen to you or someone you love—hold very important lessons and past-life connections. Extreme difficulties are often sent to teach us about such things as trust, releasing attachments, or a reconnection to Divine Source. These are so important that they often force major transformations both in our physical and eternal lives.

I saw this firsthand in the illness and death of a dear friend, whom I discussed at length in my book *Truth, Triumph and Transformation*. Pat had been diagnosed with amyotrophic lateral sclerosis (ALS), and over the span of a few years, slowly lost her ability to move. Eventually, she passed on. We had many talks about the opportunities for learning that this experience brought to her life, and Pat came to some significant conclusions.

She believed her major lessons were to let go of the need for control and her habit of worrying about what people think. These had always been significant issues for her, and she thought it rather ironic that after a lifetime of trying to control things, she now couldn't even control herself. She also asked me to tell everyone never to worry about what people think. It had been such a waste of her time, and she hoped others wouldn't have to go through something so extreme as her condition to learn the value of true self-acceptance.

These were important life lessons for her, but she believed the most crucial one was the spiritual awakening that came about as a result of her illness. She'd always practiced many types of meditation, prayer, and chanting. Yet these only became heartfelt experiences after her illness set in. Before that, she was much more analytical.

She often said that it was the *experience* of the Spirit that got her through her ordeal—and brought meaning to all the events of her life. She saw and felt the Divine presence and understood things in a way that she'd never comprehended before. In spite of her suffering, she achieved a sense of profound peace as a result of this inner awakening.

Remember that your eternal soul doesn't see earthly mortality in the same way that your current personality does. Death is simply a movement to another time and space, a short separation from family and friends. Real time—spirit time—happens in the blink of an eye, and there's no separation, for we are all connected in the truest sense.

The soul's evolution is a mysterious thing. Sometimes we can't possibly comprehend what our eternal identity may have had in mind when choosing our lessons in this life, but it's always a valuable exercise to seek that greater understanding. After all, the reason we return to Earth is to move forward. We experience pain or pleasure of any kind in order to learn, to feel, to understand, and to grow. From your soul's point of view, every experience is an opportunity. It's up to you to discover its potential and use it to bring real value to your life.

Chapter 5

WHO ARE YOU–
AND WHO ARE THEY?

Have you ever wondered what makes you *you?* What's gone into creating the type of person you are? Of course, a significant part of your makeup stems from the psychological and emotional input of your parents. We'll be dealing with those elements more in the next chapter, but it's important to remember that even your relationship with your parents may have seeds in previous lifetimes.

There are so many factors that forge a personality. The deepest elements can be revealed in our belief systems, which are the foundations of our thoughts and choices. But we're also driven by our likes and dislikes, our joys and talents, and the subtlest nuances of our long, unknown history.

Your eternal consciousness is a field of information accumulated and stored from the beginning of time. It becomes encoded with memories, personal preferences, and deeply held desires and aversions that you may not be consciously aware of. As time goes on, many of the less emotionally charged memories will fade away and more will be added. Yet even long-ago codes can bubble up today.

Let's take a look at some of the more obvious traits that can be used to identify potential past-life details. As you read about each of the following personality elements, make sure you jot down any information that you receive intuitively. Keep an open mind and heart to see how these elements could have been encoded in the past—and how they can be influencing your present.

Remember as you go through the following lists that it's important to consider both your likes and dislikes, and your preferences and aversions. A strong resistance can be as much of a past-life indication as a strong attraction. So let's review the many things that make up the tapestry of your present journey, weaving the picture of who you are.

Your Karmic Profile

If you watch the crime shows that have become so popular, you'll often find a "profiler," who amasses a storehouse of information on the suspects. They include everything from where and what the people like to eat to the types of clothes they tend to wear. This accumulation of data provides a comprehensive picture of each suspect, and even little bits of seemingly unimportant information can be revealing.

You can be your own *karmic profiler*. By becoming aware of your own natural tendencies, you can track your karmic identity and open the door to even more valuable information. As you do so, you can more easily identify which patterns you want to change and which ones you want to enhance.

Personal Style

Take a moment to think about some of your favorite things. What kind of music do you like? Are you drawn to the art and folklore of Native Americans—or to the ballets and symphonies of classic European composers? Is there a musical instrument that's especially appealing to you? Even if you haven't learned it in this life, if you love to listen to a particular instrument or type of music, it's likely you played it or were significantly exposed to it in a past existence.

Art and literature, clothing and design style, and even architecture preferences can all have their seeds in past-life experiences. If you love Asian art or are drawn to practice a religion from a different culture, you probably have fond memories of those regions. If you despise Asian art or are judgmental about foreign cultures or religions, chances are that you have some unpleasant memories relating to those locations.

In fact, widespread trends can indicate the shared karma of large groups. Even though they may not have known each other in a previous life, it's common for many people of one era to come back together. That group consciousness can then create a resurgence of interest in the culture, art, literature, and other elements of the epoch that they shared previously.

For example, in the mid-1980s, Victorian-style architecture became very popular in new construction. All over the country, people were building brand-new homes in the old-fashioned style, including wraparound porches with ornate "gingerbread" carvings and other such elements. I believe that a lot of people who had lived in the Victorian era were reborn at around the same time; and when it came time to build or buy their own homes, they reverted to a familiar style that they felt comfortable with.

I know that I myself lived in Victorian times. I've had so many spontaneous memories and triggered associations (as well as regressions) to indicate this that there's simply no doubt in my mind. I've always been extremely attached to the literature of the period, including the works of Charles Dickens, William Wordsworth, and Arthur Conan Doyle. My home is plastered with posters of pre-Raphaelite art, a wonderful school of British painters from the 19th century. Their beautiful angels, haunting themes, and compelling styles are such a part of my being that I don't know how much of it is present appreciation or past-life attachment. I don't think it much matters, though, because I believe that both the current and previous experience has touched my soul and encoded a peaceful, grateful memory.

Art, music, and food can be indicators of times and places where you've spent past lives, and so can the locations themselves. Consider the places you're drawn to—or those you've always wanted to visit.

> *What climates do you prefer? Are you drawn to large cities, ocean beaches, or white-capped mountains? Even the countries that you or your ancestors have come from can indicate past-life connections.*

I once had a client named James whose ancestors were French. His cousin's family had settled in New Orleans, and his own family had gone to New Jersey, where he worked as a contractor. He'd always loved jazz and had taken up the saxophone at an early age. When we did a past-life regression, we found out that James had been a black musician who'd lived in the French Quarter in the early days of jazz. The feelings from that experience were so profound that he now felt compelled to give up his New Jersey construction job and set out on more musical pursuits.

When he followed his encoded longing to return to New Orleans, he got a part-time gig in the French Quarter and continued his construction work in the ongoing rebuilding of the areas hard-hit by Hurricane Katrina. He now feels that he was called to the city for both purposes, and he's feeling a great sense of fulfillment in each one.

Take some time to think about all of these elements. What are your likes and dislikes where your personal style is concerned? What are your preferences or aversions in terms of art, music, architecture, fashion, cultures, and religions?

Jot down your likes and dislikes in all of these areas. What do you think they indicate in terms of location, era, and other potential elements of your past-life experience?

Even something as simple as your favorite color or your most detested food could indicate a connection. Perhaps if you're obsessed with the color purple, wearing it all the time and surrounding yourself with it, you may have been a member of royalty in a past life. If you can't stand the taste or smell of seafood, you may have worked on a fishing boat or perhaps at a seaside market, and you've just had your fill.

Work, Talents, Interests, and Avocations

What you do for a living and your outside interests and hobbies are important. Something you do frequently or on a daily basis is so consistently influential that it's very likely to have at least been suggested by an earlier lifetime. The fact is that anything that grabs hold of your time, interests, passion, or attention is a deep and often abiding part of your karma code.

Think about your talents. Is there a sport, instrument, game, or language that you seem to take to naturally? Past-life inclinations are especially apparent when an aptitude or passion occurs at an early age. Wolfgang Amadeus Mozart played the piano and even started composing music by the age of five. When someone displays a significant talent so early, it's likely that the person has engaged in that activity during many previous lifetimes. Let's not forget, however, the inspiration of Spirit. When our soul is called to create, we're often given loving guidance from unseen friends in the energetic realm.

Occupations, interests, and hobbies can be linked to each other through past-life experiences. If you're a stamp collector at the moment, you may have been employed by a post office in the past. If your present job is in landscaping, it's very likely that you've enjoyed gardening in one or more prior lives. And if you worked as an artist in a previous existence, you may have a deep desire to paint or sculpt today.

Yet longing for a certain career could also indicate an unfulfilled past-life wish rather than encoded experiences of success. I once had a client named Sara who was desperate to be an acclaimed actress. She auditioned for parts and even got a few, but never enjoyed the breakout success she so was driven to achieve. In fact, her obsession was preventing her from accomplishing anything else—and it was making her miserable. She'd lost all sense of balance and personal purpose, defining her potential for happiness only through reaching this one goal.

When she consulted me about what might be blocking her energy, I told her about one of the most important Universal Laws, the Law of Paradoxical Intent. This very important element of personal energy reveals that the more desperate we are to achieve our goals, the more our needy energy will push them away, creating the opposite—the paradox—of our intentions. If Sara were to break the grip of this law and become successful in acting or anything else, she'd have to let go of her desperation.

In order to do so, we worked on Sara's present issues of deserving and self-esteem, two problems she'd struggled with her entire life. She hadn't realized that a major motivation for becoming an actress was to prove her worth to herself and her judgmental parents. This was an important issue, but we didn't stop there. We also did a regression to see if this relentlessly urgent need could have begun at an earlier time.

We found out that Sara had indeed been an actor—a man named Robert—in a previous life. In the days before film, he'd been a handsome stage actor who'd tried to make it on Broadway, but was relegated to small parts in touring companies. As a result, he was struggling financially and was always on the road.

Unfortunately, his sweetheart was a famous actress who'd fallen for him because of his good looks—but she needed him to be wealthy and present. She'd given him an ultimatum, telling him that if he didn't make it on Broadway in a certain amount of time, she'd have to move on.

During the regression, Sara felt the desperation for success welling up within her. She could see herself as this young man, lugging suitcases and costumes, traveling from town to town on old-fashioned trains. She could hear the engine chugging and the rumbling of the rails beneath her. All the while she felt her agitation as the man named Robert—fretting about what he could do to make it big and constantly wondering if his lady love had fallen for someone else.

As we explored more of that life, she realized that her lover had moved on, and the future in that life was filled with isolation and frustration. A big sense of failure and rejection had been encoded into Sara's eternal consciousness. It affected her sense of her self-worth then, and she could feel that lingering sensation now. But there was an even more complex connection between that unhappy life and this.

Sara also came to see that the successful fiancée from that incarnation had returned as her judgmental father in this one. Although he didn't focus on her acting career specifically, he repeated and replanted the belief that she needed to be a success in order to gain his love and approval.

It became clear that Sara's soul lesson and karmic directive was to arrive at a deeper and truer understanding of her value. It was time to break through this! Sara needed to release both the emotional energy and the encoded false definition of unworthiness. She had to see the truth of her own eternal worth—to redefine herself according to her soul's identity, not her career.

She used the releasing and affirmation techniques described in Chapter 8 of this book and continued to work on changing her present beliefs. As she did so, she was amazed to realize that she really had no genuine desire to act! So she forged a new career in teaching, a profession that she truly loved. Sara pursued the lesson her soul had set up for her, opening her mind and her life to the peace that comes from releasing desperation and engaging in true self-honoring.

✳ ✳

There's interesting information to be discovered when you start to investigate the unknown history behind your career, passions, and hobbies. Take a look at your experiences in these areas. Do you have frustration? Are you longing for something different? It may be, like James, that this is the path you're meant to follow. Or it may be, as it was for Sara, a misleading desire from a past-life experience, one that holds an important lesson and a valuable gift for you. You can focus a regression process on this or any other issue. You might be surprised by what you find out.

It's All Relative

One of the clearest ways in which we can access karmic information is through investigating the intricacies and nuances of our most meaningful relationships. As I mentioned previously, it's a commonly accepted reincarnation principle that groups of people often choose to come back together. Sara's experience of reconnecting with her father to repeat her self-esteem issue isn't uncommon. We tend to reincarnate together for two important reasons:

1. We've become attached to each other in very real emotional and energetic ways.

2. We gather together to assist each other in personal evolution.

In quantum physics, there's a phenomenon called *phase entanglement.* This reveals that when two particles come together and then separate, neither can be described as independent of the other—each takes an essential part of the other particle's nature with it. This phenomenon can be found in the human experience as well. When we're with other people, we can pick up their energy, feeling affected by it long after we go our separate ways. We each have our own resonant fields that combine and connect, leaving a vibrational residue—and this is true for past lives as well.

That's why it's so important to identify the emotional and cognitive lessons that a wide variety of relationships can bring us. We no longer have to be pinballs in the arcade game of life, bouncing around from one reaction to another, entangling with people and carrying their energy and conclusions with us for all time. We can choose to heal, release, and move on.

This is the first part of healing: making a conscious intention to take control, release unhealthy emotions and beliefs, and create a new model of self-love and self-empowerment. Instead of just playing a part, we can become the director of our own movie. This is actually the direction the soul longs for. Whether we're dealing with how we spend our time, whom we spend it with, or how we let others treat us, we can muster the courage and the consciousness to move forward.

Family and Friends

Highly charged and intimate relationships such as those between close friends, spouses, and parent and child, are usually signals of profound previous experiences spent together. Dear friends—the sisters and brothers of the heart—have often been siblings before. Former family members often come back together as a unit, sometimes repeating their roles and sometimes changing them—mother becoming daughter, father becoming son, husband becoming wife.

All of these significant relationships present important lessons for us, but the parent-child connection is the most sacred of all. It's in the delicate time of childhood that our beliefs and behaviors become set. There's a heightened degree of spiritual responsibility for us as parents; and if we bring our toxic baggage into our relationships with our children, we can create a karmic pattern that may go on for lifetimes to come.

On the other side of the coin, if we've been victimized by our parents in this life, it's our clear karmic directive to release the emotions, heal the energy, and reverse the misinformation we've embraced. Our soul knows the truth of our worth and power. If we aren't given that knowledge in a healthy way in our own childhood, then as adults we must become our own loving parents, willing to give ourselves the encouragement, love, and recognition that we so rightly deserve as eternal beings.

Romance and Resentment, Love and Hate

The extreme emotions of love and hate are striking indicators of past-life connections. This is true whether the bond is romantic or any other kind. We usually don't develop intimate links with those who've been mere acquaintances in prior incarnations. Instead, we slowly weave our relationships deeper and deeper into our ongoing journey. We might meet someone and spend a couple of years working at the desk next to theirs, then in later incarnations become very close friends or even family members. Over many lifetimes, we develop even deeper intimacy, and we eventually may marry the person who was merely an acquaintance long ago.

While our connections to our parents can be the most emotionally and psychologically influential of our lives, our marriages and sexual relationships are often the most complex. Sex, passion, the rush of infatuation—when we've experienced all of these with someone before, they become almost irresistibly compelling when we meet that soul again in this life. This often explains the phenomenon known as *love at first sight.* What we don't realize is that this isn't the first sight at all. We've known this person and had some emotional—even passionate—experience together in a previous existence.

This can create some confusion where the soul lesson is concerned. Some people believe that if a connection is that profound, their destiny is to spend the rest of their lives together. They use the term *karmic relationship,* meaning that it's in their destiny to be with the person, but this is simply not the case. A karmic relationship means you've been together before—not that you have to do it again!

I once had a client who was living with a man who was verbally and sometimes physically abusive. Through our regressions, we found that this wasn't the first lifetime with this pattern. Like many women who've endured abuse in past lives, my client had little social or financial power in those eras, so she felt compelled to stay with him. She'd been willing to be dismissed, neglected, and hurt many times before because she felt she had no choice. In every life, however—including this one—the relationship started out lovingly and passionately. As time went on and her partner's violence grew, he always expressed deep regrets, and the sincere intention to change his ways.

Originally this woman thought that it was her present karma to stay with him and help him change his ways by continuing to give him unconditional love. In essence, however, she was dishonoring herself and enabling him to repeat long-held patterns. Really, the lesson was to learn how to leave him, love herself, and know that she deserved better.

They were brought together again so that she could finally make the soul-intentioned decision to honor herself. She also had to learn that this life was different, and that she was capable of caring for herself on her own. In this case, the karmic relationship brought with it a lesson of self-empowerment and letting go, but it was destined to repeat itself until that important consciousness shift was made.

Consider your relationships with family members, friends, and lovers. Do you see any patterns in how you deal with others or how they deal with you? What are the lessons you may have brought forward from previous lives? Remember, these patterns could also hold some lessons about your relationship with yourself.

Whether you feel great love or extreme revulsion toward someone, there's an important message for you in that connection. The meaning may be to stand up for yourself or to speak your truth. It could be about living in authentic power and not being a victim—or a tormentor—any longer. You have the choice to reclaim your power and evolve into a higher understanding of your purpose here. Finding and living your truth in this place and time, and in your present relationships, will make all the difference now and for lifetimes to come.

Chapter 6

SECOND THAT EMOTION!

People often ask me if we bring back our individual personalities with all of our psychological challenges and emotional makeup. A related question often is: With all of our personal problems, why would the soul decide to raise the old issues again? The answer to the second question is that if we have unfinished business and misinformed belief systems, we need to get clear—we need to rise to a higher level of truth and peace, as well as access a deeper, ongoing compassion for ourselves and others. And for this reason, the answer to the first question is *yes*—as long as we need to work on an emotional matter, we'll keep carrying it forward until it's healed or resolved.

That unresolved issue might, however, manifest in entirely different ways. As we'll see, our karmic code can cause us to play role reversals. In one life a person may be a critical brute, abusing his child into submission. The next life, he may be the kid being abused and becoming submissive.

Now, these may seem like totally opposite issues, but they aren't at all. In both cases the lesson is about authentic power. Although strictly speaking, of course, the behavioral lessons are different, the karmic intention remains the same. Both parent and child need to learn how to empower themselves authentically—to live, speak, and act with *genuine* power.

Let's take a deeper look into this kind of karmic pattern, for it's an ongoing relationship issue for many, many people today. In the case of the critical brute, his psychology causes him to seek power fraudulently by controlling and demeaning others. But his karmic directive is to learn how to live in his authentic power with civility and love, to let go of the bravado and express himself with respect. His soul longs for him to see others as equal and deserving of his compassion. In the search for soul truth, authentic power comes from within and never needs to diminish others.

In the case of the passive person, his karmic directive is also to reclaim his true, eternal strength. Although this may be difficult during an abusive childhood, it must be established at some point in order for this issue to finally be resolved. The soul's intention for the submissive person is to learn that he is worthy of his own respect—and is truly powerful no matter what misinformation he may have been given. He must arrive at his sense of authentic power by learning to speak up for himself and taking action on his own behalf. In reawakening to soul truth, he must learn that he deserves to make himself a priority. He must choose to respect himself and take the risk of insisting on respectful treatment from others.

These may be difficult lessons. The person who's chronically arrogant often believes that this is where his real strength lies. The person who's persistently passive can have fear and submissiveness so deeply encoded that he has no idea how truly powerful he is—and no idea how to express that in the world.

But until these souls are willing to let go of these skewed assumptions, they'll be unable to bring balance back to their eternal lives. They may repeat their roles life after life, or they may switch places from victim to aggressor over and over again. Either way, the opportunity to deal with the lesson of authentic power will keep reappearing until the souls take advantage of it.

This is why the parent-child connection is so important in terms of karma. First, it's the basis of our ongoing psychology, our mental and emotional patterns that persist throughout this life. It also provides the setup for our adult relationships, continuing the opportunity to either heal or reinforce the initial issues established in our youth.

Even if you separate out the karmic relevance, it's important to know the immense psychological drive this bond can create. For example, if we have a history of rejection or abandonment from one or both of our parents, we actually project that into our psychological motivation. You may have heard the phrase *We marry our parents*. This is essentially (yet unconsciously) true, because we're trying to resolve the unfinished business that originated there.

If we don't get the love, affection, or acknowledgment that we deserve from our mother and father, we actually become attracted to the same kind of distant or even hostile people who rejected us in the first place. It's an attempt to compensate for something still missing from childhood.

This effort to gain approval through association is bound to fail because we always pick someone who's as resistant to giving us love as our parents were. In this way, the karmic issue is not only repeated in childhood, it continues throughout our adult lives—at least until the soul's intention of self-love and self-honoring is persistently and positively addressed.

Karmic Psychology

We get the bulk of our psychological makeup from our mother and father, but it's possible that both our parental connections and our emotional issues are sourced in past-life experiences. Unfortunately, some people tend to use this as a reason to give up on themselves. They think that since it's karmic, there's nothing they can do, but precisely the opposite is true. In fact, coming to terms with our ongoing psychology is a big part of where our present power—and past-life healing—lies.

The truth is that we have the power to change lifetimes of patterns by mastering the emotional and behavioral problems we're consciously aware of now. Our intention to create peace of mind, self-love, and self-empowerment goes a long way toward transforming our encoded consciousness.

The beauty of this is that we're not limited to dealing with these issues by virtue of psychological approaches alone. We also have the option to investigate the karma involved, healing them on a much deeper level. So let's take a look at some of our most prevalent issues in terms of what kinds of karmic connections can be traced to present emotional patterns.

Moods, Emotions, and Personality Patterns

I once had a client named Shelly who came to me with low-grade yet chronic anxiety. Physically, she suffered from muscle tension, headaches, rapid heartbeat, and agitation—all daily symptoms that got more severe when she was in the throes of some kind of project, such as giving a big party, hosting a soiree for her husband's business colleagues, or even just planning a family vacation.

When we investigated Shelly's history, we found that her mom had always held her to the highest standards. She had insisted that her daughter do well in school, be courteous, and always present a perfect appearance. In short, Shelly's mom was a strict perfectionist, and my client turned into an exact replica.

Shelly had grown up believing that the only way to get her mother's (or anyone else's) approval was to be perfect in every way and to perform according to the imagined expectations of others. Unfortunately, being perfect is stressful; and her subconscious drive to look good, say the right things, and be the best wife and mom turned into chronic anxiety.

Her therapy had three important steps. First, she needed to express her emotions concerning both the issue and its source—her mom. She needed to ventilate the fears that her perfectionism had created, as well as grieve the lack of a loving mother, along with the loss of happiness and peace of mind that a self-accepting attitude would have brought about. Shelly also used her journal to express her anger at her mom for misrepresenting the truth of her value and for not giving her the unconditional acceptance every child deserves. This exercise wasn't intended to blame, just to vent the anger so that Shelly could get it out of her emotional makeup and energy field.

The second step was to identify and reframe the false conclusions her mother had taught her. Shelly had to release the assumption that she needed to be perfect to win approval. She also had to let go of the self-imposed demands that supported this false conviction. Her home, car, and appearance no longer had to be perfect; and she no longer had to impress every single person she met. This required my client to create a completely new belief system. She had to define herself as valuable and perfect just as she was, without condition or performance.

Shelly worked hard on changing her perfectionist assumptions. She took responsibility for the emotional quality of her life, and she created the shift in consciousness that she needed. It took work, but she felt liberated for the first time. She no longer had the chronic anxiety symptoms or the ongoing worry. She finally felt free, peaceful, and relaxed—except in just one area.

Although Shelly was much more comfortable, she still resisted letting go of her perfectionism at work. She'd thoroughly transformed herself at home and in social situations; yet on the job she was still the worrisome, performance-driven person she'd been before. She realized that this was all self-imposed because she'd never received any criticism from her superiors—at least not in this incarnation. When this last piece seemed unresolved, we decided to do a past-life regression. What we found out was very interesting.

Shelly's mom in this life had been a demanding headmaster at a school where Shelly had been a teacher in a previous existence. In a repeat of energies, Shelly was constantly bearing the brunt of the headmaster's perfectionism, always being judged for everything from her appearance and her classroom cleanliness to her techniques as a teacher and the behavior of her students.

It became apparent that although Shelly was able to release a lot of her mom's present-life indoctrination, she'd residually held on to the old encoded fears and demands concerning work. After the regression, she continued to reframe her beliefs in that arena; but we added releasing, rescripting, and affirmations in order to lay to rest that deeply encoded part of her perfectionism.

Remember, whether or not there's a karmic component, there's *always* a connection between your emotional experience and your cognitive structure—that is, between your moods and your thoughts. No matter what has happened in a past incarnation, negative feelings signify fearful, judgmental, or catastrophic beliefs. Those false ideas need to be restructured in this life, and any unhealthy conclusions from previous existences need to be cleared as well.

The duality of this energetic structure is important. If you tend to be depressed, you may have been emotionally beaten down when you were young, but there also may be lingering conclusions of hopelessness from preceding existences. Low self-esteem may be sourced in previous lives filled with criticism, but your current training is also likely to be in play. There's clearly a connection between past-life influences, present-life upbringing, and ongoing unresolved emotional issues.

It's part of your soul's intention to clear your eternal consciousness of any untruths. Therefore, pervasive assumptions such as powerlessness and unworthiness that perpetuate toxic thinking in this life will be carried forward if they aren't cleared up now. However, if you deal with things on a cognitive, emotional, and karmic level, you'll be able to cover all your bases. By releasing the feelings, clearing the karma, and restructuring your belief system into healthy assumptions and intentions, you'll not only restore balance to your personal energy field, you'll bring a dramatic new direction to your life right now and to your soul's future evolution.

What are the moods you tend to live in? What do they reveal about your upbringing and about the beliefs you're still embracing now? How can you change false past conclusions along with present toxic beliefs in order to foster a greater sense of well-being and self-esteem?

Meditate on what your thoughts and moods could reveal about possible past-life experiences. Always make the conscious intention to believe in yourself, your power, and your unlimited worthiness. This is your soul's unchanging and eternal truth.

Addictions

Similar to your emotional personality patterns, addictions can be sourced in this incarnation as well as past ones. In addition, some substance addictions, such as alcohol, also have a hereditary component. Children of alcoholics are more likely to become addicted themselves, and the layering of the potential sources actually indicates an even deeper karmic connection to this issue.

I once had a client who was an alcoholic and drank at least a bottle of wine each day. She'd tried a 12-step program, but she couldn't gain control. When we did a past-life regression, we found out that she'd owned a winery, and her addiction had started in that life. We did a rescripting, and instead of abstaining from drinking altogether, she decided to give up the wine, which had been her substance of choice in this life and that one. Although this selective sobriety doesn't work for everybody, she was able to stop the daily binges and restrict her alcohol intake to one or two martinis per month, successfully shifting that karma code.

As with alcohol, other addictions such as food, drugs, and smoking all impact our chemical makeup and influence the vibrational memories encoded in our etheric bodies. Such physical involvement compounds the emotional power of the experience, making it all the more likely to recur if we don't aggressively change that encoded pattern in this life.

Think of the addictions you may have. (Many of us have at least one.) Do you engage in too much of any substance, whether it be food, cigarettes, or drugs of any kind? Remember, your karma doesn't care if the drug was prescribed or not—overuse of anything becomes encoded in your consciousness.

Don't forget the motivation of escapism. What painful memory or emotional trauma might you be trying to get away from? There are also addictive activities, such as shopping, work, the Internet, video or online games, gambling, and sex. Could you be engaging in any of these as well? If so, what lessons are these habits bringing to you?

All of these addictions may have served to help numb your feelings, but that's certainly not the way to clear your karma. Use regression and rescripting techniques to find the past-life source of any addiction and to initiate personal healing now. Your soul longs for self-mastery, and dealing with this type of issue is one of the best places to start.

Maintaining addictions can only serve to fragment your energy. But when you release these issues in past and present vibrations, you shift your consciousness and bring balance to your personal resonance, setting up a strong foundation for immediate change. So whether you just want a happier life this time, or you want to save yourself from having to deal with it in a future existence, working on releasing your addictive behaviors is well worth the effort.

Fears, Phobias, and Obsessions

During my time as a counselor in private psychological practice, I saw many occurrences of *trauma-based phobias,* which are serious and often debilitating fears that originate in a specific personal experience. For example, when a client of mine was young, he watched his grandmother die of a heart attack, and he later developed severe hypochondria with obsessive anxiety about the condition of his heart. In this and in many other cases, we can often trace the correlation between childhood experiences and adult anxiety.

Yet there are countless examples of phobias that seem to have little or no relation to our current history. When this becomes apparent, it's very helpful to look farther back. The truth is that a surprising number of fears and phobias are rooted in past-life experiences, especially when death or serious injury was involved. A death by fire, drowning, or falling could easily result in those specific phobias in this life.

I once had a client who'd been murdered by drowning in a previous incarnation. Not only did she develop asthma and other breathing problems in this life, she also had a terrible fear of water. It became so severe that she couldn't even take a bath comfortably. Even when she put only a few inches of water in the tub, she'd always suffer an asthma attack and have to get out.

Obsessive-compulsive disorder, another anxiety-producing condition, revolves around the fear of losing control. People who have this condition try to alleviate this dread in desperate yet fraudulent ways—by washing hands, counting, or resorting to other repeated behaviors.

I once had a client who came to me with a cleaning obsession. She was unable to work or even leave the house much because she cleaned incessantly, washing and rewashing dishes, vacuuming already spotless rugs, and dusting the furniture over and over again. When we performed a past-life regression, we found that she'd been indentured to work as a very young boy, sleeping on a pallet on the floor in a storeroom. Her job was to clean all of the items in the large showroom of a fancy silversmith. Her supervisor inspected every item for dust and fingerprints, and if anything were amiss, it ended up in beatings and loss of meals and free time for this young man. Just knowing the source helped her relax, and when we released and rescripted that life, she was able to let the obsessive cleaning go.

> *Do you have any disruptive behavioral patterns—any fears or obsessions that affect your daily life? What do you think they could reveal about possible past lives? What lessons do these issues hold, and how can you start the healing process now?*
>
> *Meditate, and ask this question: What does my soul want me to do? The answer in these cases is usually to let go and trust!*

Your signature resonance is made up of many things, including your mental, emotional, and spiritual filters. Past-life investigations can help you deal with many psychological problems. Serious and ongoing conditions, however, may also need a more comprehensive approach. If you're suicidal, bipolar, or engaged in unhealthy behaviors that could cause you to harm yourself or others, then a more therapeutic model may be called for.

Allow yourself to be open to traditional and alternative treatments. Keep in mind that not every psychological or emotional problem is based in a past life. Some concerns are quite normal—such as the fear of public speaking, which is considered to be the number one phobia. Some issues are based in cultural and environmental histories. Whatever you may be dealing with, if it disrupts your functioning or your comfort, it needs to be addressed.

Let yourself explore all the elements involved, but always re-member that your soul is leading you on a path to self-awareness and self-mastery. To balance the many dimensions of who you are, it is vitally important to live consciously and awaken the love and authentic power of your core self—the essence that reaches from the eternal past to the unknown future.

Chapter 7

THE SIX
KARMIC CAUSES

The soul has some grand desires. You may not be aware of all your inner motivations, but they drive your life forward with a force that can't be denied. In fact, even if you try to resist your lessons and opportunities—whether pleasant or uncomfortable— you'll find that they'll continue to resurface. This is why it's so important and valuable to search for the hidden meaning behind your experiences. When you align your conscious intentions with your soul's motivations, a wonderful kind of magic begins to occur.

Your Soul's Path

What made you choose your career? Why did you pick the classes you took in school? There must have been something you were interested in, something you wanted to learn and master.

Your soul has the same inclination. There's a reason why it has chosen the lessons you're experiencing. Your spirit is driven by many desires, and whether they're pleasurable, adventurous, or challenging, they can be found in your eternal life plan.

> *Think about the following motivations for incarnation, and consider them in terms of the direction your life is taking. These are the six major reasons why souls incarnate, and they often hold within them the causes of your karmic circumstances.*

1. Desire

Desire is a part of life, an element of human consciousness, and a significant factor in your soul's directive. In fact, your spirit had some desires before it even started on this path of repeated incarnations. With each evolving life, those longings may have shifted; they may have been fulfilled; or perhaps they've become even more compelling and deeply encoded. Here are some of those that bring us here and keep us coming back:

- *Your soul longs to experience*—to see the vivid colors of life; to smell a spring flower or an autumn breeze; to hear a symphony or a splashing stream . . . to touch, taste, kiss, and feel.

- *Your soul longs to express itself*—to be heard speaking truth and creating ideas; to get excited by joyous revelations and beautiful interpretations . . . to sing, draw, build, and create.

- *Your soul longs to learn*—to feel and understand things on all levels . . . to emote, observe, and know *how, why,* and *what else?*

- *Your soul longs to grow*—to let go of habits; to reach beyond patterns . . . to thrive, expand, and achieve in the most profound ways.

- *Your soul longs to connect*—to share, to relate, to live in harmony, to assist and serve . . . and to love and be loved.

- *Your soul longs to arrive*—to reawaken to its eternal essence and live in its eternal truth, and to rest in the peace of Divine consciousness, whether in a physical body or not.

All of these desires are valid reasons for the soul's incarnation, and they can formulate the basic meaning and deeper motivation in any experience. When engaged in the higher desires, such as loving expression, connection, and compassion, the more positive energies and vibrations of life will be encoded in your karmic intentions. If, on the other hand, the lower vibrations of desire (those that are ego driven, fear based, or overly attached) become the stronger forces, then it's possible that more difficulties can become encoded.

In its purest state, desire isn't a bad thing. Every great advancement in science has been fueled by the appetite for knowledge. Every significant work of art or musical composition was driven by the longing for creativity and expression. Every meaningful relationship, whether with friend or lover, is fueled by the desire for companionship and camaraderie. And finally, every act of kindness, from a single favor to far-reaching humanitarian acts, is driven by a compassionate urge that far transcends the simpler forms of what we tend to desire personally.

These purpose-driven desires can create real joy that is meaningful and long-lasting. But when elements such as fear, attachment, and ego are introduced, karma can take a different turn. For example, it's perfectly natural to seek a loving relationship. Yet if we become frantic for love because we're afraid of being alone or because our ego needs it to feel secure, then we've attached something fearful that becomes a part of our karmic code. This is an important consideration, for attachment turns desire into desperation, a highly charged emotion that creates imbalance, blocking the very things we're longing for.

So what do we need to do to keep our karma clear and our longings pure? *Unattached desire is enjoyment without addiction, pursuit without fear, and accomplishment without ego.* There's purity in this kind of endeavor that sets the soul free and creates a pervasive peace of mind. But when we attach an unhealthy meaning to any of our dreams, we can set ourselves on the path of some very enlightening karmic causes, such as repetition, compensation, and retribution.

2. Growth and Learning

The soul takes many different paths and evolves through many different rites of passage. Just as we encounter many lessons throughout our school years, our soul faces unlimited opportunities for growth.

This is, after all, the eternal plan: to keep experiencing and moving forward, to continue arriving at new levels of understanding, and to keep assisting others in their process as well. Each new situation is another class . . . each new issue is another project. As we advance to levels of truly higher learning, we begin to perceive life in a different way. Instead of measuring ourselves only by significant events and major acquisitions, we can move into the soul's point of view and measure ourselves by our eternal value.

This places the difficulties we experience in a different perspective. Instead of remaining powerless victims, we can become enlightened observers. Throughout it all, we need to remember that the soul never intends to suffer just for the sake of suffering. There's always a lesson, a gift for us or for someone else, a transformation into something far greater.

Even in deep grief there is value—or there can be if we allow ourselves to move through it with awareness. Pain and loneliness often force us to look inside and go deeper. We can ignore that opportunity (and many people do); but if we're willing to experience the emotions, feel the grief, ventilate it, and then ask the right questions, we'll be able to utilize the experience in order to move on.

Many lessons can be carried in one pervasive issue. Such was the case when a client named Karen came to me to find out why she'd been so blocked in her love life. Although she'd dated, she had never been in a serious relationship that lasted any length of time. When we investigated her history from this life, we found that her father, although a good provider, had been emotionally distant, always physically present but personally unavailable. As is always the case with detached, neglectful, or abusive parents, self-love was a part of Karen's life lesson.

My client had grown up longing for her father's affection and attention, feeling she was nothing without it. She needed to let go of this false assumption and reclaim a sense of her authentic value, a typical lesson in self-love. Karen's soul longed to live in her beautiful truth, and she found that her intention to do so was very healing. When she let go of defining herself through her father's indifference, she arrived at a far greater peace of mind and sense of self-acceptance than she'd ever had before.

In addition to dealing with these present issues, we did a regression to release her deeper blocks to love. Karen found out that her current father had been her husband in a past life. This is actually one of the many classic patterns of relationship returns. He'd had much the same persona in that time, having been a wealthy merchant who was absent and indifferent and who'd married her late in life.

In that existence, Karen had spent her youth worrying that she'd never marry. Through her late teens and 20s, she'd suffered judgmental looks from her female friends who were successfully married or engaged. She'd been as desperate for a relationship in that life as she was in this one, but for different reasons. The solution at that time seemed to appear when a widowed, wealthy merchant proposed to her.

When the wedding finally occurred, she was very happy; and she attached her worth and even her self-definition to her marriage and the financial security it brought about. Having a husband had become so important that she'd ignored the fact that he was indifferent and dismissive. For the rest of that entire life, although she was unhappy with the relationship itself, she sought validation from the outer world through her marital status and the material superiority it brought. Ironically, even though she'd been condemned for being single, she used her own wedded state as a way to judge and demean others who weren't as fortunate as she.

Karen realized through our work that her desperation and overattachment at that time—along with her later judgment of the unmarried people around her—created the karma code that contributed to her current frustration in love.

She did a karmic rescripting, visualizing herself feeling confident and worthy even when she was unmarried. She also viewed herself having compassion for the single girls around her, letting go of judgment of any kind. Karen also rescripted her childhood from this life, determining that from now on she would be her own loving parent. She ventilated her feelings of rejection from her dad and let go of striving to gain his love and approval.

Perhaps the hardest part was releasing her present desperation for a relationship. But Karen chose to be responsible for her own happiness, and she was glad that she now lived in a society where a woman doesn't have to be ashamed of being single. Her release of urgency liberated her, allowing her to finally give herself the love and approval she'd always been seeking from potential partners. She became genuinely happy and projected a joyous vibration, a sensation that was very new to her.

This is an important case because it so thoroughly represents the complexities of life. Karen had read some books on attraction, and although she visualized attracting love—and on an *intellectual level* believed that she deserved it—she was consistently frustrated. She hadn't realized the power of the hidden fears and desperation that had been encoded in her consciousness. Her decision to do all that she could to heal this primary issue of self-love meant that she'd no longer have to face it in countless repetitions of similarly difficult experiences. She shifted her daily life force, changing her results both in this incarnation and in others.

3. Karmic Repetition

The spirit's intentions resurface over and over again. In fact, the soul's choice to repeat is one of our strongest karmic causes. It's easy to see why we'd want to repeat the gratifying experiences, such as truly loving relationships and enjoyable talents and hobbies. Yet our repetition doesn't stop with the good stuff.

It may seem surprising, but we can be equally attached to negative influences and difficult times. When an extreme bond is formed, a more highly charged emotional state develops. In this way, the more fiercely held habits—whether healthy or not—become deeply encoded in our consciousness, compelling the soul to come back to repeat the experience. Eventually, however, the personality will be called upon to release the toxic attachments and reestablish balance and pure motivation.

Let's look at some of the ways in which our encoded patterns of *repetition* manifest themselves:

— **Pleasurable activities.** The wonderful sensations of our senses are joyously encoded and repeatedly calling us back. When we don't take the time to appreciate simple pleasures such as the beauty of a sunset or the taste of a piece of fruit, we are failing to honor one of our spirit's primary intentions. The soul wants us to know that we may be missing an opportunity, and these seemingly small episodes really represent the finer moments of life.

— **Repeated addictions.** Sometimes a seemingly pleasurable experience can become so habituated that it directs the momentum of our entire life. Whether we're addicted to sex, drugs, food, or anything else, the desire for familiarity and escape becomes irresistibly compelling. That habit then becomes encoded and gets carried with us into future existences. One of our greatest tasks is to release these extreme patterns and redefine ourselves by the peace and strength of our sacred identity. Until we realize that our addictions block our spiritual connection and reinforce false priorities, we'll be bound to repeat them in increasingly difficult ways. The lesson here is to let go of the substance and return to the Source.

— **Personality patterns.** It's not uncommon to return with the same type of personality we've had before. For instance, if you've been taught to be passive, it's possible that this is the state you've become accustomed to in previous lifetimes, and you'll continue to repeat the pattern until you learn how to stand up for yourself. If you tend to be a caretaker now, it's likely that you've been so in the past—and with some of the same people. It's important to get out of your archetype, however. Breaking out of your personality mold can be one of the hardest things you may have to do in this life, but it's absolutely necessary if your old way of being doesn't resonate with your spirit's path toward balance, honoring, and enlightenment.

— **Repeated relationships.** Sometimes we come back with the same people purely out of the desire to repeat a lovely journey. When there's passion, support, love, or tenderness, it's not unusual to want to reexperience that. But we also tend to repeat relationships that are uncomfortable, unhealthy, or even abusive. These types of replications are partially stimulated by our familiarity with the people involved, but they also come from the soul's desire to learn the lesson that connection brings. Whether we're staying in a dishonoring situation out of fear, past-life obligation, or deeply indoctrinated habit, it's incumbent upon us to investigate our real motives. Our soul's ultimate goals are truth, self-love, and impeccable honor. Whatever old pattern may be keeping us stuck, we can release the attachment and arrive at a higher relationship with our true selves. Remember . . . sometimes the karma—even in the most compelling personal connection—is learning how to let it go.

I discovered this last element of karmic repetition firsthand when dealing with one of the most emotional experiences of my life. Remember when I talked about my first regression, and the young boy's death due to pneumonia being a source of my asthma and respiratory infections? I didn't know it at the time, but that wasn't the only connection that this long-past experience had to my present life.

About 20 years later, I was in the process of adopting two children. My husband and I were looking at foreign orphanages in order to find older, harder-to-place kids. We'd decided to adopt two children at the same time so that they could be there for each other to make the difficult transition easier.

After years of research, we found an orphanage in Saint Petersburg, Russia. In the long process of identifying children, I'd seen countless pictures and videotapes. I finally identified a girl, and because there were no sibling groups available at that time, we were looking at boys from the same orphanage.

In reviewing the tapes, I had an immediate reaction to an eight-year-old boy named Sergei. There was an instant recognition, a deep connection with a longing to reunite. Given the thousands of pictures I'd seen over the previous three years, I'd never had such a reaction before. I started the paperwork to adopt Sergei, along with my chosen daughter, Vica.

I was convinced that we had a long connection and that Sergei was the right choice. I knew we had past lives together, but at first I hadn't realized that this was the little boy who'd passed away when I was his nanny. Although I hadn't thought about that existence in years, when I meditated upon our hidden connection, the experience immediately came to mind. It was clear to me that this was the boy who had died of pneumonia. He came to me now at the same age that he'd left me in that incarnation. I was ecstatic that we were going to repeat our loving connection, and I thought, *I'll give him the life I took away from him then, and our karma will be resolved.*

This conviction made me even more convinced that this particular boy was a part of my destiny. I continued to meditate on it—as I always do with important decisions—asking for Spirit's guidance. Over time, I started getting uncomfortable feelings during these meditations, and I asked what they might mean.

The answer I received from Spirit was very disappointing but unmistakably clear: *This beloved child may have died in your charge, but it's now time to let that relationship go . . . along with the guilt and the responsibility you've been carrying.*

I was surprised to receive this kind of clarity in my guidance from Spirit, but I was still resistant to hearing the truth. Just a few days after this meditation, however, something happened so that I could no longer deny what the Universe was trying to tell me.

The Russian adoption agent asked me if I was still considering Sergei. When I said that I was, she told me that she had important information about him. The social worker at the orphanage had recommended that Sergei be brought into a home where he'd be an only child. She said that he'd recently developed some significant behavioral problems, especially with respect to mistreating the girls in the orphanage. She told me that our new daughter Vica would have a very difficult time if we insisted on adopting Sergei as well.

I thought about the message in my meditation and knew that I had to let Sergei go. No matter what happened, I never needed to hold on to that guilt. Now it was necessary for me to release the boy along with that responsibility and self-blame. Somehow I also knew that this choice was necessary for Sergei's process as well. What we really needed was a *karmic disconnect*.

The adoption agent then recommended another little boy whose video I hadn't seen because he was in an older age group. His name was Jenyaa, and he became our son—a tender, witty, and fun-loving addition to the family whom I'm so deeply grateful for. In fact, I can't imagine any other boy as my son.

I now know beyond a shadow of a doubt that the destiny for my husband and me was deeply encoded with these two wonderful children—even though they were 11 and 12 years old when we adopted them. It was absolutely essential in terms of our souls' evolution to embrace these children and let Sergei go.

Repetition is driven by our familiar feelings, even if we can't always identify or understand them. We do, however, have it within our power to rise above the drive for familiarity and to arrive at a healthier place where honoring, not habit, is our sole (and soul) motivation. In the eternal scheme of things, there's real purpose in every coming together and in every parting.

---

4. Karmic Compensation

The pattern of compensation becomes a karmic cause when an extreme experience in one life causes us to overreact in another. In this case, a strong desire to reverse the energy of past experiences makes us go too far in the other direction. This adjustment will often be so extreme that it creates the polar opposite experience in this life.

Let's take a look at some of the more common reasons for *karmic compensation.*

— **Compensatory addictions.** Although present addictions can come from patterns of repetition, they can also result from the energy of compensation. It's not uncommon for people with weight problems to have previous lifetimes where they didn't have enough to eat. The constant hunger from the past becomes so encoded that it now seems impossible to feel full.

Be careful about the emotional energy you put around this or any addiction, however. If you always feel guilty when you eat, that strong emotional resistance could encode intentions to stay away from food in a future life, bouncing you right back into a situation of hunger or even starvation. Whatever present compulsion you may have, whether it's caused by compensation or repetition, it needs to be addressed and released. Both extreme attachment and resistance are healed through balance and self-mastery. This is true for anything you long for or avoid.

— **Perpetual longing.** Yearning is a primary karmic cause for compensation. If an unhappy or uncomfortable condition exists for an extended period of time, a desire for its reversal takes hold. Since any perpetual wish becomes encoded, it can create unexpected circumstances in your next life.

For example, a client with a severe case of agoraphobia began to work with me after she'd been housebound for several years. Every time she tried to go out alone, she had a panic attack. In addition to applying classic therapeutic techniques, we did a regression to find out what deeper sources might be hidden. We discovered that in a past life she'd been a traveling salesman, needing to be away from home almost all the time. During the regression, she saw herself in boarding houses and old-fashioned hotel rooms, wishing to be home with her family. Every time she had to leave on another trip, she told them, "I wish I could stay home."

In her present life, she developed agoraphobia at the same age she'd gotten the sales job. That wish to "stay home" had been so emotionally charged for such a long time that she developed a debilitating condition making it impossible for her to leave.

In cases of compensatory longing and karma, the old adage is true: *Be careful what you wish for, because you may get it.* It just might not be in this life, or in the way you would prefer.

— **Compensating for an extreme imbalance.** Although addictions may fall into this category, there are many other types of imbalances that could cause karmic compensation. Let's say you had a life of leisure where you didn't work at all and were waited on by servants. If you had little or no regard for others, you could come back in a position of servitude. In cases such as this, the compensation isn't a result of the experience itself; it comes from your attitude. And while indifference or ignorance may lead to a lifetime of compensation, hostility and judgment lead us into the next karmic pattern, that of retribution.

5. Karmic "Retribution"

Both compensation and retribution represent an energetic pendulum swinging from one extreme to another—with one important difference. Compensation is a reversal of energetic experience, while retribution is a return of your own outgoing energy; and it almost always has something to do with the way you've treated people in the past. This is your soul's intention to learn what that vibration feels like.

Retribution is *not* punishment, despite often being defined in this way. Where karma is concerned, the concept comes more from the root word *tribute*—to pay. Don't let this confuse you, however. The Universe isn't paying you back for misdeeds of the past; rather, you're energetically paying it forward. In other words, how you treat and view others now will be how you yourself are treated and viewed in future lives.

The force of this energy in your eternal life will often manifest in the form of role reversals, where two people take turns giving and receiving highly charged treatment until that cycle is broken. Although it manifests most often in parent-child or husband-wife relationships, this back-and-forth pattern can happen between any two people who've had emotional encoding with each other.

For example, if you have a domineering and arrogant boss, it's entirely possible that in some past incarnation, you were in a position of authority over him, giving him the same type of treatment. This emotional dance could then occur lifetime after lifetime, with each of you switching roles as the resentment and anger builds and becomes more deeply encoded.

The pattern will stop when at least one person lets go of the emotion and chooses the path of authentic power. It's not about winning or losing. From the soul's point of view, it's a matter of arriving at a more enlightened attitude toward every relationship we encounter.

Let's look at some other patterns of retribution:

— **Parent-child relationships.** This is the most sacred of all bonds, the one in which individual psychology and self-esteem are formed. Children are open vessels, longing for love, yet ready to receive any kind of treatment that's given them. Don't let this upset you, but if one or both of your parents were critical, neglectful, or abusive, it's entirely possible that in a previous life, you were the parent sending that same energy in their youthful direction. Being mistreated in this life charges you with resentment and the desire for revenge, encoding an intention to pay back the experience. But you don't need to hold on to that code—or the emotions involved. If you've suffered, the lesson is clear: You deserve to be loved and you definitely deserve to love, acknowledge, and value yourself. Become your own loving parent, ventilate the feelings, and let the old resentments go.

— **Romantic relationships.** Marriages and romances can experience much the same back-and-forth role reversal. Emotions run deep where love is concerned, and intentions can become deeply encoded. Just as a longing for affection can cause repetition, rejection and rage can cause retribution.

This was the case for a client of mine named Julie, who came to me to find out about her past lives with her present husband. Their relationship was volatile, with lots of power struggles and bitter arguments. They were both always trying to prove themselves right and get their own way. Although Julie found it impossible to be happy, she also found it difficult to leave.

We did several regressions, and the information we received was very revealing. In their most recent life together, Julie had been the husband, a mean-spirited factory worker who came home expecting his dinner to be on the table and his wife to be silent. In that life, Julie had wanted and gained all the power. Before that, her husband was again her husband—this time a hard-working farmer who demanded that Julie work just as hard to prove her worthiness as a wife. There were other lives as well, back-and-forth power struggles where the couple returned to each other in order to make one more attempt at control. Although it was unhappy and unhealthy, they were both entangled in a deep need to stay together until someone won.

But life isn't a matter of winning or losing; it's about enlightenment, and in each existence comes the opportunity to raise yourself above the patterns that deny your spiritual truth. Although Julie and her husband had the same issues, they kept switching places, paying their mistreatment and false motivations forward, destined to do so until at least one of them saw the truth and the cosmic silliness of it all.

One very important lesson that's commonly found in relationship retribution is the need for compassionate treatment and a sense of equality for both partners. This may seem stunningly simple, but it's so easy to be indoctrinated in our false bids for power and superiority that the option for compassion and caring simply slips away. Yet whether you're the victim or the victimizer in this life, you can wipe that karmic pattern clean. Let go of the need to pay someone back for mistreating you, release those who aren't ready to move on, and embrace a new life of peaceful self-love.

— **Prejudice, judgment, and inequity.** Retribution can also result from your social attitude toward individuals and groups. Judgment, unkindness, or outright hostility will create a deep scar in Universal energy and in your karmic profile. In fact, there's one thing that you can guarantee where karma is concerned—that which you judge, you *will* experience.

I've seen countless cases of this kind of karmic retribution throughout my practice. I did a regression with a client named Fran, who came in to deal with weight-loss issues. She'd been very heavy for most of her adult life, and although she'd tried many different diets, she couldn't seem to drop the unwanted pounds. When we did her regression, we saw that she had been a beautiful young woman during the Roaring Twenties. She had been very slim, with short hair and a stunning beaded dress, in classic flapper style. When she saw herself being asked out by a heavyset man, she laughed in his face and told him that she'd never be seen with the likes of him. She also had a close friend in that life whom she judged and criticized for being overweight. Seeing this, Fran realized the irony of it all: "Skinny people don't understand what I'm going through now, just like I didn't understand or have compassion for heavy people in that life."

This process helped Fran in three important ways. First, she was able to release self-condemnation concerning this issue, and her newfound self-compassion actually made it easier for her to lose weight. Second, she was able to forgive those who were judging her. When she heard the comments or saw the scornful looks, she remembered that she had once been that way; and she said a prayer that those people wouldn't have to go through what she was experiencing. Finally, the regression made her realize that she hadn't really let go of her pattern of judgment. In this life, however, she applied it to a different issue.

Fran was a very smart woman, and she'd spent much of her time looking down on those whom she perceived as being less intelligent. She knew it was both compensation for her weight and a repeated mental pattern that her soul longed to release. She vowed to let go of all judgment, and to see people as equals no matter what they weighed or what kind of job or education they had.

William experienced another case of this type of role reversal designed to bring about an important lesson. He was a handsome young black man who was well-to-do and very popular in the local media. He consulted me in order to investigate his energy and find out what was blocking him from moving on to a national level in terms of professional success. He was a spiritual and open-minded man, and in our very first session he told me about a recurring dream in which he was a white plantation owner in the Deep South in what seemed to be the early 1800s. He lived well and had many slaves, both working the land and in the household. He told me that he thought this was a dream of a past life when he was white and had actually bought and sold people of color. He felt so strongly about it that we decided to go deeper.

In his regression, he could see himself riding out to the fields late in the day, watching dozens of tired black men toiling away. Although he wasn't the type to beat his slaves, he was a stern businessman, indifferent to the slaves' plight. He saw himself at a square where slaves were bought and sold, and although he knew that his transactions were breaking up families and separating loved ones, he didn't seem to care.

This regression saddened William to the depths of his soul, but he could see the retribution patterns in his own life. He'd grown up in poverty and prejudice and had also endured much separation. His father had abandoned his family; and when his mother died, he was shuttled from one home to another. Even as an adult, he often found that he had to leave family members and friends in order to move from town to town in search of increasingly better media jobs. Yet many of the best positions were given to Caucasians.

As is typical, the roles had been reversed. As the plantation owner, he had power and was resented by those he controlled. He now believed the candidates who surpassed him in today's job market were his slaves from that past life, and he was determined to let go of his resentment. He also had to forgive himself for the residual guilt hanging on from his previous incarnation.

Then he told me something that surprised me . . . he said that he also had to stop judging black people. When I asked what he meant, he said that for most of this life, he'd had the tendency to look down on anyone with darker skin than his own. But now he knew that his lesson was to let go of all resentment and prejudice and to see himself and everyone else as equal. He meditated on releasing the energy of separation, and he focused on opening his heart to harmony and unification instead. He felt that he was no longer that white plantation owner or a black media personality, but a mixture of both.

Every human being has experienced multiple lives. We've all been black, white, male, female, fat, thin, servant, master, smart, and silly—many times over. When we learn to love all of our differences, we see the heart of each individual, and we're able to learn what others have to teach us. Regardless of our apparent variations, we must all arrive at a real understanding of our mutual Source. No matter what we are in any given life, the one identity—the Divine Spirit—that links us all will always whisper the truth and peace of our eternal connection.

6. Service

Service is a compelling motivation for the soul. It's one of the greatest expressions of love; and when it's genuinely offered, it projects one of the highest vibrations. In its purest state, this is a genuine, unattached longing to promote good in your life and the lives of those around you. But there are times when your karma presses you into service out of the need to learn and grow.

Motivation is always a key ingredient in your karmic causes, so it's important to keep that in mind when reflecting on your choices. For example, the desire to be admired or congratulated can often be a subconscious motivation to assist others. In such cases, it's the attitude—not the act of service—that encodes an energy of need rather than love in your eternal consciousness. So if something you're doing is ego driven, even if the deed is good, that act will be tainted with a negative vibration, creating a potentially difficult karmic code.

In addition, helping others can also be fear based. Don't confuse genuine acts of service with behavioral patterns of people pleasing.

The need to gain approval in this way is born out of fear of rejection. In this case, your intention is motivated by the sentiment, *I have to do this in order to be accepted.* This is a distortion of your soul truth, for you deserve to be accepted just the way you are.

Let's take a closer look at the types of service and their karmic causes.

— **Karmic service.** Sometimes your intention is a reaction to experiences from past lives. If you saw people suffering yet refused to help, your soul may compel you to serve humanity more fiercely this time around. If you were critical or brutal, you may come back to aid others. Or if you've had previous existences filled with feelings and behaviors of entitlement, setting yourself above everyone else, your attitude of self-service and dismissal could stimulate a strong desire to be of greater assistance now.

— **Personal service.** When you have a loving, honoring connection with the people around you, extending care becomes a natural thing to do. Unfortunately, if this hasn't been the case in past lives, the role may be forced upon you now.

This was the case for my client Gabrielle, who came to me after her brother had been in a car accident and became paralyzed from the waist down. Since her mother was elderly and her brother was unmarried, it fell upon Gabrielle to become his caretaker. She fed, clothed, bathed, and entertained him; and she arranged her work schedule around his needs.

When we did a past-life regression, Gabrielle saw herself as her brother's mother. In that life she hadn't been very maternal, though. He had been her only child, but she'd been too self-involved and interested in social climbing to care much about him. She saw many domestic scenes where she either dismissed or ignored him, sending him off to play on his own or asking the nanny to distract him. Gabrielle realized that because of her unloving heart at that time, her soul gave her another opportunity to be of assistance to the soul who'd once been her son and was now her sibling.

That regression created a consciousness shift for Gabrielle. She was able to care for her brother without the resentment she once had. But she didn't overcompensate out of guilt. Instead, she was able to create balance by hiring help. Rather than being a burden, she found that the hours they spent together were filled with joy and loving connections.

— **Sacred service.** This is found in the unattached giving that goes out to the world. Your lovingly tendered time and energy will expand to create a vibrational momentum of gratitude. The energetic truth is that we are all connected. What happens to others can't be separated from what happens to you; so when you work to restore balance, peace, and harmony in other people's lives, you bring a greater store of those qualities to yourself.

This purely intended and wide-ranging service is truly one of the highest purposes for the soul's incarnation. Such heartfelt longing preceded your karma code but may have been silenced for quite some time. If so, you may be ready to reawaken that deep internal voice. Bring joy to others and you'll reverse the karma of self-absorption, encoding a new and vibrant energy that will return more joy to you.

Live in balance and engage in service that comes genuinely from your heart. As your spirit evolves, the inclination to serve will grow within you. Honoring yourself and others will raise your resonance and be in harmony with all of your soul's directives.

*"You are led through your lifetime by the inner
learning creature, the playful spiritual being that
is your real self. Don't turn away from possible futures
before you're certain you don't have anything to learn
from them. You're always free to change your mind
and choose a different future, or a different past."*

— RICHARD BACH, *ILLUSIONS*

PART III

Releasing the
PAST,
Healing the
PRESENT,
and Freeing the
FUTURE!

Chapter 8

DECONSTRUCTING MISERY, RECONSTRUCTING JOY

by Tom Cratsley

Many years ago I was confronted with stubborn reactive patterns in myself and my clients, and I pondered this idea: If we do indeed create our reality through our thoughts, then we ought to be able to *un*create our mental habits—even those in the unconscious mind. We just need to find out how we came up with them.

In my search, three thinkers influenced me greatly: Robert Fritz, for his pioneering work on structural thinking and the creative process; Roberto Assagioli, the great Italian psychiatrist and creator of the psychosynthesis process; and Andrew Jackson Davis, a 19th-century American mystic and prophet who developed a model of the human psyche based on levels of perception.

I explored a number of techniques and discovered that a simple, focused regression could bring unconscious source material to the surface. Although it can be helpful to have an objective person assisting in the process, it's not always necessary. The regression on the CD accompanying this book is a focused regression process that can be done on your own—*at the place and time you find most convenient for pursuing a specific issue you long to heal.*

When working directly with clients, I ask them to go back to the first time they ever experienced the conflict they're seeking to resolve. The thought of their present discomfort is the only stimulus they need for the unconscious to reveal its contents, and the regression is often immediate. Without exception, clients find themselves in the midst of traumatic memories—chock-full of emotional, mental, and physiological information—and these often appear to be past-life scenarios, although I give no specific direction to regress that far.

The steps for emotional release that I describe in this chapter should be applied at the time that the traumatic past-life memory is reawakened, whether using the CD accompanying this book or any other method. By applying the following approaches, you'll be able to clear your discomfort and declare newly empowered conclusions and intentions.

This moment of emotional shifting is an important time. By making key decisions in the presence of old memories, clients can relieve themselves of the pressures contained there and create a new and liberated relationship with the event. In the process, they're also able to call back the personal power and resources that were surrendered in the helplessness of the original trauma. In essence, they're able to transform the meaning of the experience from pain, fear, and limitation to confidence and freedom.

While there's controversy over whether or not past-life regression experiences are real, the debate is irrelevant when it comes to the healing they produce. I personally believe in the karmic process and the path of the soul; but if for some reason these memories aren't genuine, then it's even more wondrous to think of how such dynamic healings occur. The mind spontaneously produces intricately textured and layered metaphors that accurately reflect the workings of the psyche and consciousness, making the positive transformation more meaningful.

Healing Trauma

Thousands of these regressions have taught me a great deal about reactive patterns. First, they have structural integrity.

Trauma and its related thoughts are locked into memory by intense emotion. Unless the strength of those feelings is clearly identified, as well as the associated thinking, it's difficult to address the issue effectively. However, when thoughts and emotions are pinpointed and deliberately let go, the subconscious responds, and the event itself is neutralized. Similarly, when definitions, conclusions, and responses to the incident are named and released, the mind creates an entirely fresh and liberating perspective on the original experience. This newfound power over the situation means that the subconscious is no longer compelled to react negatively to similar situations.

Second, the trauma of origin often has significant pain or injury associated with it. That physical anguish can be carried forward in varying degrees, even from one lifetime to another. As Sandra has described, the encoded information manifests in the part of the body where the trauma took place, a cellular memory forming a present-life condition.

Such was the case with my client Bob. His issues centered on betrayal by a business associate who'd disappeared after taking a considerable amount of money—setting back a project that Bob had devoted three years of his life to. This left him depressed, angry, and spiritually shaken. He also experienced a stabbing pain in his back, behind his heart, as well as extreme pressure in his jaw.

During the regression, my client fixed on an experience that had occurred when he was barely two years old, when his father had come home in a drunken rage. Bob was upstairs and, hearing the commotion, he went down to investigate. His father grabbed him, slammed him against the wall, and held a knife to his throat. He was paralyzed with fear and confusion.

During this session, it was revealed that Bob's father had been a World War II commando. Scarred by his experiences, he had wild behavioral swings and frequent angry outbursts. In addition to releasing the physical effects of this particular early incident, Bob cast off his feeling of helplessness. He also let go of his need to always be on guard—especially around men—for fear of being overwhelmed and betrayed. Finally, he released the conclusion that relying on and trusting in other men would only lead to disappointment and disaster.

After Bob cleared this childhood trauma, his inner guidance directed him to a past life where he was a peasant who had been killed during an uprising. He'd been run through from behind by a knight's sword, and he needed to release his rage against authority and government, as well as the fear of being annihilated by anyone who claimed to be in power.

Bob let go of these emotions and the conclusions they carried. He then declared himself open to his spirit's capacity for knowing how to stand tall in his truth. Even when interacting with people in authority, he declared that he could still be safe and effective. At the close of the session, he reported feeling freer, without the long-held pain in his back or jaw.

The Art of Letting Go

To successfully release our limitations, it must be understood that serious constraints are defined multidimensionally. They aren't just ideas of what we can't or shouldn't do; they're infused with intense emotion, physiology, and context—which is the map of the traumatic experience. This includes elements such as spatial relationships, textures, aromas, and the sequence of events. When releasing, it's important to have significant awareness of these pieces of the puzzle and their relative importance, in order to give the unconscious mind a reference and clearing point.

Whenever we experience pain, there's always a desire to have it removed, and the reason the mind can't respond favorably is because *it was never given the direction to create discomfort in the first place.* Physical suffering is the side effect of internal contradiction. If key elements of the conflict are understood and released, the pain will be cast off. For this reason, wounds and injuries from the past that are manifesting in the present can also be eliminated—first by bringing the originating source to light, and then by consciously directing the body to release the tangible effects while engaged in this source experience. Carol's story illustrates this process.

In her early 60s, Carol asked for help with lifelong pain in her lower back. The source appeared to be an existence where she was wounded by a wooden spear in battle. She spent the remainder of those years on Earth wandering alone, in pain and despair. She was able to release the emotions and physical effects, and was pain free for more than five years.

Carol then returned with a new set of concerns. She'd experienced a mild stroke the previous year and had been nearly housebound ever since. Irrational fears, anxiety, nausea, and depression were her daily companions. In the session that followed, she saw a lifetime where she witnessed the destruction of her home and community, as well as the deaths of everyone she cared about.

She was overwhelmed by feelings of helplessness, confusion, despair, and shock. The sight of such horror was physically nauseating and left Carol with a number of reactions, including survivor's guilt, hatred for God, and a strong death wish. But having identified the source, she released the emotional and mental debris from that memory, and her nausea vanished. She then felt free to move around without the fear of losing all that mattered to her. The seemingly irrational and amorphous dread suddenly had clear meaning, which enabled her to both understand and transform her internal (and encoded) experience.

The Power of Presence in Defusing Old Traumas

The most critical element when endeavoring to release un-wanted emotional and mental patterns is the capacity to be as thoroughly present with them as possible. Misery is often a jumble of feelings and thoughts, and it can be difficult to clearly identify what you need to let go. For instance, fear and anger are central to most issues, but vary from one situation to another. You must be able to name them with greater accuracy to effectively clear them. Fear of what? Anger at whom or what? Once labeled, you must feel the fullness of each emotion as you are releasing it.

Follow this initial step with a deep, full breath, along with the intention to let go of the emotions or thoughts as you ex-hale. When the heavy, negative feelings have been cast out, use positive declarations and affirmations to summon your resources and establish more harmonious patterns of behavior and thought. Indeed, clearing the energy makes room for positive patterns to emerge.

In addition, the importance of any resistant habit is measured by the emotional intensity of the source experience. The uncon-scious tends to respond more readily when the depth of feeling is matched by an equally powerful desire for change. To help you on your own journey, the following case is a more detailed example of specific, highly effective choices that one client made while re-membering a source trauma.

Ken came to me looking for support in healing a lifelong fear of intimacy. In tracing his frustration to its source, he found himself in ancient China, seriously wounded in the midst of battle. His entire village was under attack, and he saw his wife being killed while he was helpless to do anything. He crawled off into the tall grass and watched in agony as all that he loved was destroyed. Although he survived, he was left isolated, bitter, and depressed. He spent seven years as a beggar, endlessly taunted by those around him. Then he was arrested, tortured, and killed for being a vagrant.

Ken's experience was one of profound guilt and acute self-recrimination. He knew that he had to let go of these feelings and the conclusions they engendered. These are some key choices and declarations he made during our session:

- *I release the feelings of guilt I still carry over not being able to save my wife in that life.*

- *I ask her forgiveness, and I forgive myself.*

- *I release the feelings of self-hate and self-disgust, and the conclusions of cowardice that I still carry for not being able to save her or anyone else.*

- *I release the feelings of shock, grief, and despair that I carry from that time.*

- *I release any conclusions I may have made that I am unworthy of the love or trust of others—or that I am likely to let them down.*

- *I release the physical impact on my body from having been wounded and tortured in that life. I release any of the effects I may have carried forward to my current body.*

- *I open myself to my spirit's capacity for knowing how to attract and maintain an intimate, loving relationship— one that is mutually nurturing, supportive, and safe.*

Weeks after the session, Ken found himself feeling much more comfortable about making connections. He had let go of fear and was willing to consider that it could be safe to let love into his life. In addition, he noticed that he was walking more easily, whereas he used to limp. He attributed this to releasing the effects of the torture he'd experienced in that past life.

Many Lives, Many Ways to Freedom

It's not uncommon to have fleeting memories of intervening lives between the source trauma and your present experience. These could involve similar injuries, physical problems, or emotional struggles. When the original ordeal is cleared, however, all related experiences can be recalibrated and neutralized as well.

This happens as the mind sorts out the new meaning of the first event and the significance of all similar, subsequent incidents.

Recurring painful memories can be an opportunity to address structural resistance in the unconscious mind. If patterns repeat after you've cleared one trauma, you may have to go back in order to see if there's an even earlier source event. By immersing yourself in the memory, and by identifying and releasing the emotions and limiting thoughts, the impact of these recollections can be minimized and even neutralized. Remember to take a full, deep breath following each release.

When you're successful, you'll sense a significant shift in your relationship to the memory, and often feel physically lighter. Upon completing the releases, it's valuable to declare yourself open to new resources of healing and self-empowerment.

Use the following list to help release and clarify emotions and their corresponding thought patterns, keeping in mind that it's only intended to be a guide, not an exhaustive inventory. Often, the words you choose yourself can better represent your internal experience. Use your intuition to come up with your own declarations and affirmations, considering your present-life patterns as well as any information you get while doing your regression.

Releasing Emotions

I release feelings of [see below] that I carry from that time.

Helplessness, hopelessness, despair	Unworthiness, insignificance, inferiority
Confusion, shame, embarrassment	Abandonment, betrayal, rejection
Isolation, loneliness, separation	Persecution, being trapped or unwanted
Anger, hatred, rage, resentment	Powerlessness, inactivity, victimization
Self-hatred, self-disgust, self-dismissal	Contempt, disgust, judgment
Jealousy, envy, lack, impatience	Pride, superiority, self-righteousness
Guilt, responsibility, caretaking	Fear of death, life, or God
Fear of specific situations or specific people	

Releasing Strategies

I release any need I had to be or feel responsible for others (including my parents, spouse, friends, and relatives). I release them to their own resources and their own spirits.

I release the need to:

- *Control or be in control*

- *Be special or different*

- *Be perfect or prepared*

- *Look good, or look or be any specific way*

- *Be loved, accepted, or approved of in any certain way*

- *Be responsible, or know everything in advance*

- *Suffer or be punished*

- *Seek revenge*

Releasing Conclusions

I release any false conclusions I may have made as a result of these emotions or events. I release any misinformation or limitations about my:

- *Purpose, power, or wisdom*
- *Worth, value, or deservingness*
- *Intellect or capabilities*
- *Strength or courage*
- *Physical body or self-image*
- *Specific relationships or sexuality*
- *Spirituality*

I release any conclusion I made that it is unsafe for me to experience:

- *Love or intimacy*
- *Power or leadership*
- *Truth or knowledge*
- *Spirituality or physicality*
- *Feelings or opinions*
- *Any other aspect of my being*

I release any belief or conclusion I may have made that:

- *I am inherently flawed, imperfect, or a failure*
- *I am (or others are) untrustworthy*

- *I (or others) need to be controlled*
- *I do not have the capacity to . . .*
- *Life is unjust or a struggle*
- *Evil triumphs over good*
- *There is no room for me in this world*
- *There is no support for me in this life; I am alone and on my own*
- *It is better not to have what I want rather than risk the pain of losing it*
- *The material and spiritual worlds are separate*

I release all that I have said or done to support these conclusions in my life.

Declarations

- *I ask forgiveness for . . .*
- *I forgive myself for . . .*
- *I forgive others for . . .*
- *I open myself to my own true strength.*

- *I open myself to the strength and support of others.*
- *I open myself to my spirit's capacity for the free and full expression of:*

Love	Creativity
Leadership	Sexuality
Power	Physicality
Knowing and perceiving truth	Communicating my truth

I open myself to the free expression of and the capacity to know:

- *My true nature and purpose*
- *My own true strength and authentic power*
- *The strength and support of others and of the Universe*

I open myself to my true relationship with:

- *My own spirit*
- *God*
- *The earth*
- *The people sharing this world*

- *The living spirits, angels, and guides*
- [Any specific others]

All of these affirmations and declarations are designed to reverse the misery remaining from past traumas. When you open yourself to the emotions there, you can release them and replace the old conclusions with a higher truth and a joyous strategy for life.

Chapter 9

REWRITING
YOUR CODE

Take a moment to reflect on your life. Which patterns would you like to turn around? Do you think there's something you could be repeating or compensating for? Perhaps you've started to get a picture of who you are—and who you've been. When the facts about the past come into view, you have a much clearer perspective concerning your purpose and plans. You also possess a far greater power to heal the present and redirect your future.

In the previous chapter, Tom Cratsley gave you an overview of his powerful approach to healing today's issues. The combination of experiencing, releasing, and affirming while becoming aware of past influences can reverse core issues in your code. The resulting shift in your eternal being will create a dramatic transformation in all kinds of results.

Since your consciousness creates your reality, it's important to go deeply into all that it holds. Once you discover the hidden information from your long-unknown past, you'll be able to release the blocks that have been holding you back, freeing you to move forward without the old constraints and encoded false conclusions.

Significant present-life changes can result from this process. When the mysteries of your soul's intentions are revealed, personal and Divine purposes align, creating a vibration of balance and synchronicity that the Universe finds hard to resist. Your soul's evolution longs for healing; and when it comes to releasing and rewriting your karma code, there are four steps that are essential:

1. Awareness of the source, pattern, or meaning of the lesson

2. Releasing and rescripting negative experiences, emotions, or attachments

3. Shifting encoded conclusions and karmic intentions

4. Learning the lesson and applying it to the present

Each step is vitally important, so I want to expand on them as they relate to some very interesting cases.

Step 1: Awareness of the Source, Pattern, or Meaning of the Lesson

As we've discussed, there are many ways to access past-life information. You may even get help from a guide, a process that's explained in detail in the next chapter. But whether it comes through regressions, readings, or any other manner, the data is vitally important.

You've read about many people who've had great revelations regarding previous incarnations. In some cases, finding out what happened was the only thing necessary for healing. It's important to know, however, that you don't have to be aware of every single life that relates to the issue you're dealing with today. In fact, there are even patterns that can be reversed without any karmic investigation.

When you genuinely learn the lesson, it satisfies soul intention and ameliorates any karma encoded in related, yet still-unknown, past lives. If a problem is persistent and keeps popping up, however, it could be a sign that there are other opportunities with related past lives that still need to be addressed for total resolution.

This ability to return to the past whenever you desire can be very valuable. In fact, this is what the regression exercise on the accompanying CD was designed for. Using that process, which is described in Chapter 11, you can retrieve potential source information regarding any issue and reveal the deeper meaning behind the present problem.

Diana's Dilemma

Diana came to see me when she started feeling mounting panic over driving alone. She'd had some driving anxiety when she was much younger, but that had long since been resolved. In fact, when her worries returned at the age of 42, she used her old techniques of relaxation to try to work it out, but to no avail. Her alarm was at a heightened state when she came to me to find out if a past life could be involved. So we did a regression to work on Step 1, finding out what happened—and what it might mean.

Diana's regression took her to a crowded street in a large city she believed to be in Poland, circa 1920, where she was driving alone in an old-fashioned car on a busy thoroughfare. She was turning left, stuck in traffic, when she saw a trolley barreling down on her. With no option to move the car and no time to get out, she died in a mangled wreck.

The meaning was clear. This was a trauma-based phobia, and the accident had occurred at the same age in that life as the age in this life when Diana began having these recent panic attacks. In fact, the closer she'd gotten to her actual age at that event, the more frequent and severe the terror had become. But just uncovering this information relieved a great number of her symptoms. Still, she knew she had to continue going through the steps to reverse her panic entirely.

❋ ❋

When you get the details, give yourself time to process their meaning. Consider your present life to see how it all fits together. Let go of any blame, guilt, or victimization; and trust the information you get.

Try to see things from your soul's point of view so that you can find the valuable lesson in the experience. When you do, you can use all of the steps to clear your code and change the influence it has on you now and in the future.

Step 2: Releasing and Rescripting Negative Experiences, Emotions, or Attachments

When you consider the many lives you've had, it's amazing to think of all the emotions and energy you're carrying—even if you're not aware of it. Letting go of these encoded feelings is vitally important if you want to make a complete karmic release and shift your present and eternal consciousness. This stuck energy actually blocks the flow of your life-force vibration, creating obstacles to healing, romance, and even wealth that could be coming your way. And since the old, unhealthy resonance often gets stuck in your chakras—the main energy centers of your body—it's often helpful to do chakra-clearing and balancing meditations in addition to your regression and rescripting techniques.

Pattern Prisons

When you start to look at previous incarnations, it becomes very clear that emotional attachments are extremely strong forces in your personal code. But if those patterns aren't broken and released now, they're likely to become even more deeply embedded and problematic. This requires addressing your past-life events with clarity, perseverance, and focused intention.

Unfortunately, we can become attached to anything, including people, habits, and feelings—good and bad. *Karmic attachment* usually means we've been emotionally involved with these issues before, and it's time to take them seriously. In fact, releasing unhealthy emotions and stuck patterns is one of our greater karmic directives—far more important than making a lot of money or acquiring lots of material objects.

Our patterns imprison us, even if they're of our own making. Feelings of fear, longing, or depression, although uncomfortable, can become oddly safe and familiar, creating their own kind of momentum in our lives. But releasing difficult emotions and rescripting our karmic history will lay the foundation for present change and future happiness and success.

This rescripting—or rewriting—of the source experience is a vital part of the second step. (And there's a track on the CD accompanying this book that takes you through the process.) According to the space-time continuum, all time exists at the same time. The future is vibrating in pure potentiality, and so is the past. Just as you can go forward and create different designs in the days to come, you can also go back and rewrite endings for the scenarios that seem to be keeping you stuck.

These *new* intentions for past experiences can be extremely powerful. Many people have told me that upon doing a rescripting —along with the other steps here—they found their present situations to be rapidly changing. One remarkable case happened in a seminar I gave several years ago, where a man who'd been smoking for 40 years did a regression to discover the source of that habit. He didn't reveal the origin to me, but he later told me that our rescripting and releasing had helped him break out of that pattern prison. After smoking for four decades, he was finally able to quit!

You can make some radical changes, too. They may take a little longer, but your health, happinesss, and enlightenment are well worth your time and attention.

Diana's Solution

Although Diana started resolving her anxiety about driving as soon as the cause was revealed, she had to release and rescript as well. She did some letting go during the original regressions, but she also revisited the experience, casting off more of the panic and bringing peace to the situation. She changed the event, visualizing the traffic clearing ahead of her; and she saw herself driving out of the way before the trolley got too close. She then envisioned herself living a long and healthy life, driving comfortably all the while. She transferred that image to this incarnation, affirming that driving alone was safe and comfortable, and very soon she felt completely relaxed with it.

When you suffer from a condition as dramatic and physical as panic attacks, it's your body's memory trying to tell you something. Anger, dread, and trauma may be influencing you without your knowledge. Find out what it is; release and rescript it; and move through the process until you get results.

All of the steps of consciousness recoding will help you follow your karmic directives. Your soul wants you to clear your eternal consciousness of its unhealthy codes and patterns. A dynamic piece of the puzzle is rescripting the experiences of your past so that their toxic emotions and conclusions can be replaced by far healthier ones. The progression through this and the following two steps are key ingredients in releasing you from the prisons of your own mental, physical, financial, and relationship patterns.

Step 3: Shifting Encoded Conclusions and Karmic Intentions

It's clear to see how the emotional experiences from past lives can leave residual conclusions that may be unhealthy, so we must release these toxic assumptions along with any unwanted *karmic intentions* that may be lingering.

Your karmic intentions are the personal motivations that have remained embedded from previous incarnations. They may be driving forces in your life, even if they're diametrically opposed to your present desires. Some people use the term *karmic contract* to describe this phenomenon, feeling as though they're locked into these old choices for the entirety of this existence—but most karmic intentions don't have to be binding. With patience and persistence in rescripting your karmic code, you can rid yourself of past-life wishes that no longer serve you.

Such was the case for a woman who attended one of my recent seminars and asked me if I could see a karmic source for her present infertility problems. The details came so quickly and clearly —and the emotions were so visceral—that it was immediately apparent how and why this issue had become encoded.

I saw the woman in what seemed to be a rustic cabin. She was busily engaged in the many tasks of a pioneer mother, hauling water from a well outside, cooking at a large fireplace, and caring for the multitude of children surrounding her. It seemed as though there were at least eight children all under the age of ten; and although the older kids were trying to help, there was a lot crying from the little ones wanting to be fed and attended to.

As I moved through this scenario with this woman, I could feel the resentment overtaking me. Although she wanted to love her children, she was exhausted and overwhelmed. In her mind, I kept hearing the intentions: *I don't want any more children. I can't have any more children.* As an adjunct, she also repeated the conclusion that she had to protect herself from having sex with her husband—that it just wasn't safe to go on like this.

This is a clear example of karmic intentions creating present realities. Because of her conclusions about her husband, I asked her if she also had issues concerning sex and intimacy in this life. She laughingly responded, "Only with men!" So her encoded conclusion that sex with a man could only lead to more misery manifested in her being a lesbian this time around.

In addition, her karmic intention not to have any more kids was still locked in, blocking her desire for children in this life. And although she felt no desire to change her sexuality, she was driven to release the old limiting intention so that she could indeed have a family now.

In order to make that happen, she had to rescript that past-life scenario, seeing herself with just a few children, lovingly providing for them and not feeling overwhelmed. Whenever the resentment or fatigue popped up during the process, she needed to make releasing affirmations, intending to let go of those emotions and reactions. She also had to declare that it was safe and comfortable for her to have children, and that she enjoyed her life with them.

She affirmed her openness to receiving children in this life, rescripting her past-life relationship with her husband by setting sexual boundaries that he was willing to abide by. In doing all this, she reclaimed her power and neutralized the hidden resentment that had been an unconscious but compelling factor in her infertility issues. She released the past and was finally able to change that code, and soon she had a beautiful baby boy—in spite of the fact that she only had one ovary!

Resentment is a driving force in our unrevealed karmic intentions, creating destiny directions that we no longer want. It almost always results in lifetimes of compensation. Consider these three common issues and the karmic responses they create:

1. Resentment toward children: childlessness or having to deal with difficult offspring

2. Resentment toward work: difficulty getting a job or
    attracting jobs you don't like

3. Resentment toward men or women: difficulty finding
    a healthy and happy relationship

In short, hidden resentment toward *anything* either pushes it away or attracts it in a very difficult package. This and other negative emotions and intentions must be released in order to establish the freedom to get your present desires met. When you let go of the animosity, you can create a new code of safety and self-empowerment. In addition to clearing the karma regarding this issue, however, it's also advisable to look at any resentment you're feeling now. What kind of intention could you be encoding for your future—both in this life and beyond?

Whatever you need to release, whether it be from a past life or a present circumstance, heartfelt affirmations can move your healthier intentions forward. Don't just pay lip service to these new ways of thinking and feeling, though. Do a heart-centered meditation on their meaning, breathing in the energy of their truth. Mindless repetition of positive statements won't have the power to shift things the way that experiencing the beneficial emotions of empowerment and truth can.

Many wonderful affirmations and declarations were explained in the previous chapter, but the following list can be helpful as general intentions for shifting your karma. In addition to using specific intentions that apply to each unique past-life issue, you can use these affirmations at any time to initiate changes in your code.

- *I release any old, unhealthy habit or conclusion. I release any past desire that limits me in any way.*

- *I have free will and I make my own choices. I no longer need to respond according to any hidden intentions. I release them and let them go.*

- *I am free from the past. I leave any toxic pattern, thought, or attachment behind.*

- *I bless the past and let it go. I am free.*

- *I open my heart and mind to a deeper connection with my spirit. I release false codes within my eternal consciousness and return to my Divine Source and identity.*

- *I am physically, mentally, and emotionally free. I am whole and healthy. Divine consciousness fills every cell.*

- *Divine energy moves through my eternal life, releasing the past, healing the present, and blessing the future.*

- *From now on I choose freedom and self-empowerment. Each day brings greater enlightenment, purity, purpose, prosperity, and love.*

- *I open my heart to understanding the lesson that my soul longs for me to learn. I have all the strength and resources I need to move my life forward in a blissful and purposeful way.*

These are just a few of the affirmations that you can use to turn things around. *One of the important purposes for using these affirmations is the reminder that you now have the power, free will, and resourcefulness that you may not have had in previous experiences.* You don't have to respond in the old ways anymore. You can deal with anything, and you always have the option to do things differently. Using affirmations will help complete your karmic reversal when you apply your new intentions to your present issues. This is an important part of Step 4, and cannot be dismissed.

Step 4: Learning the Lesson and Applying It to the Present

Once we understand that our karmic lessons are issue related, we're free to completely redefine ourselves and our lives. It's not necessary to reverse every single episode, only to encode a different perception with healthy conclusions of honoring and self-empowerment. This application of past-life lessons to current experiences is an important part of the process, for the present is where the learning takes place.

There's an old adage that says: "To learn and not to do is not to learn." This is true for our karmic experiences as well. Although it's interesting to get the facts and helpful to release the past, unless we carry the meaning through to our present life, we aren't really shifting the code to the degree necessary for our purpose. After all, if we understand the simultaneity of cause and effect, we know that our current experiences are not only effects from past incarnations, but also causes for future ones. It's incumbent upon us, then, to become conscious and directive today. Moving with intention and action right now creates a new and healthier code for the future.

If we're going to heal at the deepest levels, we must investigate our unresolved issues and unfinished business. *Bringing change to the present is really one of the primary purposes of finding out about past lives—not just the events within them, but the meanings, conclusions, and expectations surrounding those events.* The challenges and difficulties will stop when the issues are resolved and these old codes are broken. But you must practice the new truths in the real world and muster the courage to bring your new intentions into your everyday life right now.

Coding Freedom

As I've discussed, one of my pattern prisons has manifested in repeated respiratory issues. Although I've been able to rid myself of the problem for many years at a time, it still comes up occasionally and forces me to deal with unfinished codes and unresolved conclusions.

Don't fault yourself if issues keep recurring in your life, too. Deeply encoded physical, mental, emotional, financial, and relationship patterns *can* be beaten. You have to be willing to attack them at every level, however. With patience, persistence, and a little help from Spirit, you'll be able to work these things out, creating a new, healthy path to a dynamically different future.

I recently had a resurgence of my challenges in the form of persistent pneumonia. I did some regressions and found that I had two previous lifetimes where I was imprisoned. One was a very long time ago—perhaps the Dark or Middle Ages. I saw myself chained to a wall in a dank, musty dungeon. The other was at a later time, and I was once again in a stone cell—this time with bars on the door.

I realized that this pattern had been a literal and figurative prison for me, and it was time for me to break free. The difficulty breathing in those horrible cells had been encoded in my cellular memory, but it was a metaphorical prison as well. In those lives I'd concluded that I was powerless to change my situation. That decision was still encoded, but it was no longer true for me. *This is so often the case for the problems we carry—we're living the remnants of a past-life lie!* I needed to release my sense of powerlessness in those times and find out what was going on now to trigger this resurgence.

First, I rescripted both of those prison experiences, seeing myself striding out of the cells and away from confinement. I saw myself stepping out on a fine, sunny day; breathing deeply; and being so appreciative of the clean, fresh air. As I did so, I affirmed: *I am free to go and do whatever I want—whenever I want,* and I happily walked away. And in the process, I knew that I had to affirm that this was true for my present life as well.

At first it was hard to see how this applied to my current circumstances. I didn't genuinely feel that I was being restricted in any way. But as I looked deeper, I realized that my limitations were self-imposed. I had once again moved into an *unconscious habit pattern* as opposed to a *conscious balance pattern.* Once more, without even knowing it, I'd slipped into the reactive pattern of working too much.

I love all of the aspects of my career: the writing, the speaking engagements, and seeing clients; and because I love it, I often get swept up in the momentum of the tasks involved. The book deadlines, lecture schedules, and private appointments—all of which I truly enjoy—were directing my time and energy. I realized that my soul had been longing for more family time, more private time, and just plain fun. In short, I had to get out of my self-established prison of an unbalanced life yet again.

I have to say that I was resistant to this lesson at first, largely because I actually do perceive my work to be so much fun. But I repeated the rescripting a few times, continuing to affirm the intention to free myself, to breathe easily, and to break the pattern of unconsciousness in my life.

I did the rescripting, but I also knew that I had to support these intentions with my behaviors. So I cancelled appointments with some clients—not just because I was sick, but because I wanted to show the Universe that I prioritized my own health and my life. This was very difficult for me, raising the old issue of responsibility. I didn't want to disappoint my clients, but I had to realize that it didn't honor them to dishonor and dismiss myself. And reestablishing balance was absolutely necessary for both my well-being and my life lesson.

In addition to taking some time off, I scheduled a cruise just for healing and fun. I took an extensive course in energy medicine given by Donna Eden, and it was an enlightening and transformative experience. This was another departure from my pattern. In recent years, I'd traveled so much for speaking engagements that I had never taken a trip for personal purposes or for pleasure alone! I realized that I *had* unknowingly imprisoned myself in an old reaction, and the pneumonia was the gift that helped me release those past lives, change my present choices, and shift deeply encoded energy.

Life Lessons

The things that keep repeating themselves are important reasons for our soul's return. These persistent, nagging issues remind us of our *karmic directives*—the life lessons we're meant to resolve this time around. We mustn't feel victimized by our lessons, and we have to remember that our soul gave them to us for a reason. What we do with these challenges, however, is totally up to us. If we look at our soul's purpose with willingness and receptivity, we can make great strides in the life we've been given now.

Of course, as I've stated, not every difficult thing that happens to us is a result of some karmic trauma. Our spirit has cycles of growth, learning, and higher intention that span the past, present, and future. Some of our difficulties are based in this life only; some are simply soul cycles, directives that are designed to push us to the next level in our eternal path. Whatever the source, they won't be deterred. Keep this in mind when reviewing the following life lessons, and consider which ones you may still need to work on and what might help you restore your karmic balance:

— **Authentic power and value.** Many people seek fraudulent power through brutality, arrogance, bravado, or even dependency; many others simply give theirs away. Neither of these approaches represents the truth of your genuine value and eternal power. Since your soul can't abide living in these lies, it will be important to find out where such false ideas came from. Rescript the originating events (from childhood input to past lives) and release their conclusions. Then figure out what you can do to set them right in this life. Muster up the courage to let go of any false feelings of superiority or inferiority. Until you do, you're likely to bounce from one to the other, seeking interesting opportunities to find your authentic truth.

— **Love and compassion for self and others.** This is one of our highest intentions and greatest lessons. The ability to love without conditions and live with caring and compassion creates a monumentally positive code in our eternal consciousness. Always remember, however, that this starts with the self. In fact, self-love is one of our most prominent and important lessons. Most of us are compelled to choose it and live it in a self-taught sort of process. Rescript the nonloving episodes from this life and others, and embrace the choice to care for yourself at every opportunity from now on.

— **Nonjudgment.** This is an extension of love and compassion. When we judge someone, it moves us out of harmony. That imbalance is then encoded in our eternal consciousness, creating the karmic intention to come back to experience the very energy we've condemned. In this way, we can experience the situations and feel the deeper emotions of those we were once critical of. Remember that judgment is a very powerful code, one that creates this unbending karmic directive: *What you judge, you will live.*

— **Awakened appreciation—releasing envy and dissatisfaction.** Envy and judgment are similar causes, both of which have fragmenting energy. Yet so many people spend their whole lives in dissatisfaction, always wanting more and wishing they have what others do. This negates many opportunities for genuine appreciation, expanding a consciousness of lack that can send your destiny in some pretty dark directions. Ask yourself: *How grateful am I for what I have—and how happy am I for other people's success?* When you let go of envy from this and past lives, it opens the way to creating an irresistible code of gratitude and magnetic life-force energy.

— **Nonattachment.** Although it's never unhealthy to genuinely love someone or something, we need to remember not to invest all of our emotion, worth, happiness, or self-definition in that person or thing. In fact, being overly dependent on something in this life may mean having to come back and live without it—or be more heavily addicted. Rescript and release extreme attachments from the past, and bring a conscious intention to releasing them now. The ultimate solution is a joyous self-definition, seeing everything external as an enhancement to an already happy life.

— **Peace, harmony, and physical and emotional balance.** Balance is often achieved by releasing attachment, but there may be other lessons involved. Prioritizing self-care and a healthy lifestyle are often karmic lessons. Reducing conflict with others increases harmony, while releasing the struggle within us brings inner peace. The key is the realization that we can master our thoughts and choices. Rescript conflicts from the past. Choose peace and harmony now to encode a higher vibration that will create better results in this life and in those to come.

The word *karma* comes from the Sanskrit, meaning "action." The active changes you make now can yield dramatic and immediate results. No matter how deeply entrenched your patterns may be, you can heal them at the most profound levels of your soul. Revealing the hidden past and rescripting those long-held codes brings amazing power to your life, allowing you to break free and move forward with an ease and direction like never before.

Chapter 10

GETTING TO KNOW YOUR PAST-LIFE GUIDES

by Sharon A. Klingler

What a beautiful world of help, love, and inspiration you have! Uncles, aunts, parents, siblings, children, lovers, friends, and teachers—all of them are here for you right now—in spite of the fact that they may have died in 1943, 1812, 1578, or even 2,000 years ago. These are the guides in the spirit world from your past lives who care for you and work with you still. They are many and varied. Besides your family members, friends, and even business associates, you have spiritual teachers and creative mentors, as well as the Ascended Masters and angels. There are spirit guides of every stripe, stemming from lifetimes that span the ages.

Why do these past-life people return to you in present times? Are they attached, trapped, or obsessed with you? Not by any means. It's very simple, really. Just as the loving relationships you have now continue after the death of the body, so do those from the past. Of course, not every single past-life connection from every previous incarnation will be seeking you out now. After all, everyone has his or her own sense of purpose, plans to make, and goals to achieve. Still, there are those who are reconnecting with you at this time—each for their own reasons.

Getting to know all of these glorious beings requires the same energy, focus, and perspective that you need in order to work with any spirit guide and in any intuitive-development practice. And the most important element of all is trust.

In working with spirit, you must learn to trust every subtle nuance, sensation, impression, idea, and symbol. You may not know what they mean, but you need to build trust in every instance. If you second-guess, doubt, or invalidate your perceptions, you'll be giving rein to your left brain (where questioning and judging reside) and closing the door to your past-life guides and present teachers.

You can practice cultivating trust both in your communication with spirit and throughout your daily life. It's similar to building any habit: the more you do it, the easier and more instinctive it becomes. And then you'll be able to do it even more! So listen to your own spirit and your guides, past and present. And *know* that what you know is true.

Why Past-Life Guides?

Why would anyone want to put so much effort into learning how to connect with spirit guides from previous lives? The past is over. Shouldn't we let it be? If there were difficulties back then, wouldn't it be better not to rake up the muck?

As you learned from the other chapters in this book, it's rarely (if ever) beneficial to ignore difficulties or suppress your painful emotions—whether they're from the past or the present. But even if you're committed to releasing history and growing through your karmic lessons, why make the effort to connect with spirit in order to do so?

It's not any more necessary to access your past-life guides in order to work on your karmic lessons than it is to engage a lawyer when signing a contract, go to a doctor when you have questions about your health, or seek out family members in times of trouble or joy. None of these interactions may be essential—but they are, indeed, vastly important and extraordinarily helpful. All of your spirit people (whether from the past or present) are here to help, guide, and love you. So why not cultivate your relationships with them? They're here for you now and always. And they all, in their own ways, bring unique gifts, histories, talents, and purposes to the table of your life.

Spirit people from the past are very much like those from the present. Past-life mothers and grandmothers will come to assist you with your current "mother" types of relationships. They'll also help take care of and watch over children and grandchildren. Colleagues will often lend a hand with business ventures, and previous spouses will help with present loves. All of your past-life guides can be your spiritual teachers and helpers—radiant beings from the higher realms.

Regardless of the special favor or talent each of them holds for you, they all share a common goal: to help you discover, heal, and release past events and traumas in whatever way they can. So get to know them! How much easier their task—and how much greater your evolution—if you open the door to their presence and discover the great insights they bring!

A Team Effort

Even as you become more experienced in discovering what your past-life guides have to share, your task in healing your karma doesn't end there. You must seek to understand and change the underlying beliefs and emotions that are linked to your karmic history. These spirit helpers can help you navigate the maze of events, but you must do the work of understanding and letting go.

Still, just as they say, "It takes a village to raise a child," it also takes a team to raise a new you. And that group includes you, your own spirit, and your spirit guides and teachers (present and past). In addition, consider the people you know currently who may have past-life histories with you, and who now bring the lesson (whether pleasant or unpleasant) home to you.

Sometimes, as a medium, I get to be on the team, too. I can help my clients discover and understand parts of the process, but it's still up to them to make the changes necessary. In karmic lessons, there's no cheating on the homework or tests!

Meeting Your Past-Life Guides

When you start to take actions to know spirit, you throw open the door for all of your spirit people to come closer and become more clearly present in your awareness. Your past-life guides are ever-present, just like all of your other spirit companions. Let's take a look. . . .

Who's There?

Close your eyes now and quickly see or sense a past-life spirit guide standing to your left. Know him or her absolutely. Completely sense the clothes, the stature, the gender, and even the feelings of this being. Trust every spontaneous nuance you perceive. What message does this spirit share with you?

If you had difficulty sensing this guide at first, you'll find—with practice—that each time you reach out to your guides, you'll grow stronger and stronger in your perceptions. All you have to do is relax and:

1. Stay out of your left brain—no doubts, second-guessing, or invalidating thoughts.

2. Stay in your receptive, imaging right brain, allowing yourself to be aware of every intuitive perception.

3. Trust everything you experience—from the strongest image or idea to the subtlest nuance of mind or body.

This is all you need to do—whether you're making a quick connection with your guides throughout your day or working with them in meditation. Let's try one such visualization now. If you'd like, you can record the following process to listen to later, when you're in a more deeply relaxed state.

Visualization with Your Past-Life Guides

<u>Introduction:</u> Close your eyes, and begin to feel yourself relax. Take a deep, cleansing breath, and release. Take another very deep breath, and release.

As you let go of all tension, you can feel yourself go into a deeper and deeper state of relaxation, allowing your breath to come and go easily. Begin to count from 3 down to 1. With each count, you will find yourself moving deeper and deeper into relaxation.

3: Feel your shoulders, arms, neck, head, and face smooth out, let go, and relax. With every passing breath, you move deeper and deeper into that point of light at the center of your being that is your eternal, invulnerable, and imperishable self.

2: Feel your chest, your back, and all parts of your body relax and grow heavy. You drift easily now into that beautiful interior light—that self who knows all that you need to know and trusts every answer, image, and thought you perceive.

1: Totally relaxed, you now rest easily in your all-knowing eternal self, the part of you that perceives every nuance and image without second-guessing or doubt.

Journey: As you remain relaxed, you begin to feel a presence. It's a radiant spirit somewhere near you, a being who has been with you often—both in previous lives and in the space of timelessness between them. Feel this loving spirit approach you now. Even if you don't see or experience every detail, allow yourself to feel this wonderful entity's presence now.

At first, you can sense a beautiful energy as this being gently lays his or her hand on your shoulder. Just take a moment now to see, feel, and sense the wonderful embrace of this loving presence.

Now watch and sense as this being takes your hand. In your imaging, you feel yourself rise up and walk together, and he or she takes you down a long corridor. It may even feel as if you're floating. Let yourself be led down this beautiful hall of many doors.

The door you're walking toward leads to the past life that you need to know the most about at this time. Your guide opens it, and together you step into that place and time where you were together before. As you do so, you notice that your clothes change and your body changes. And so do your guide's. Just let yourself step into that past life now.

You stand fully there. The corridor is gone, and you are completely in this past-life place and time. Take a moment simply to be there. Look down at yourself and notice your gender, your body, and what kind of clothes you're wearing. Notice everything about your guide, too.

How old are you in this past life? Are you a man or a woman? Trust and know the first answers that come to mind. Now see or sense the terrain around you. Where are you and what is the climate like? Is it warm or cold? Rainy or dry? Night or day? Notice the vegetation as well. What kind of plant and animal life do you see?

Take in the details as you and your past-life guide begin to walk down a path to a place where you lived or worked before. And while you walk toward this place, your guide shares with you an understanding of your relationship in that life. Was this person a spouse, parent, child, friend, teacher, or spiritual guide? What were your feelings for and about each other? Feel the connections as you continue to proceed down the path.

Soon you come to the place where you had experiences that impacted you. The relationships or events there not only influenced who you were then, but also who you are now. Your guide follows as you enter this place. And whether it is a cave, church, Victorian home, or hut, allow yourself to enter this place where you lived or worked. As you do, you immediately sense what has happened here and how it was significant in your life. Take a few moments now to gather information about this place and any event that happened here.

How do you feel in this space? What transpired, and what does it mean? Are others with you, and could they be those you know in your present life? Let yourself trust what comes to mind as you take some time to explore this time and place.

Begin to finish this up now. Take a very deep breath and relax even further. And wherever you are in your past life, you begin to see another spirit approach. This is a new past-life guide who comes to you now. This beautiful being of light is a past-life spiritual teacher who has a strong and loving commitment to help you in your evolution, your spiritual work, and your greater purpose.

With a simple raising of his or her hand, this higher guide takes you immediately to the past life where you worked on a spiritual path together, where his or her insight and teachings took you to a higher truth and sense of knowing. Suddenly, you are there completely. Allow yourself to see and sense it all, experiencing it in every way. Where are you? Are there others with you? What are you doing, feeling, and thinking?

After you take some time to see and sense everything, this guide takes your hand and begins to walk with you back to the present lifetime. You come fully back now to this present moment. As you do, take a moment to consider your current existence. Ask yourself what unwanted patterns are still taking place today. Just let yourself notice the first answer that comes to your mind. Do you recognize any negative experiences from your past lives continuing in your childhood or adulthood in this incarnation? If so, with whom did they occur? Are they still playing out? Are there any harmful actions and feelings that continue over and over that are left over from the past? Your spirit guide will give you the answers to these and other questions.

Consider what thoughts, affirmations, and new actions you can bring to bear in your current life that can help you change these patterns once and for all. Think of an affirmation, and even just one action, that can replace your old unwanted thoughts, actions, and patterns; and let your Spirit guide help you with that, too.

Closing: *Now begin to count slowly from 1 to 3. As you do, become more and more conscious of all the parts of yourself that are in the here and now, yet remembering completely every little detail from your past.*

1: Bring yourself back easily, gently. Feel your shoulders, arms, back, and chest, remembering the insights you have gained.

2: Feel your body completely as you return to this moment, this life, knowing you can make important changes now.

3: You're all the way back now, opening your eyes when you're ready, feeling a happy and renewed connection with your past-life guides who still love and care for you today.

Navigating the Course of Past-Life Discovery: A Case Study

As you can see, your past-life guides are very much like cruise directors on your voyages to the past. They not only guide you to the location and time, but they also inform you about the incidents that create karmic lessons.

Recently, in a reading for a client named Joseph, I was asked if there was a cause in a previous incarnation for the discomfort in his ankle. Immediately, I saw a past-life guide of Joe's who was dressed in a naval uniform. I also perceived the image of the two of them on a great-masted ship. They were engaged in a lot of frantic activity and there was urgency on the deck—whether due to a storm or a battle, I couldn't tell. Joe was dressed as a captain, and the past-life guide beside him seemed to be his second in command. Suddenly, a great beam the size of a tree trunk came crashing down from the sails high above, knocking over the captain (Joe in this lifetime); breaking several bones through his body; and smashing his lower leg, ankle, and foot entirely.

So much physical damage was done, including the necessary amputation of his mangled leg, that Joe permanently lost the life he loved at sea. He spent the rest of his days landlocked, unfulfilled, and very unhappy. He'd defined his purpose, happiness, and fulfillment by his freedom to travel the world and command a ship. He needed a new definition of self, a different understanding of freedom, and a fresh sense of purpose—none of which was forthcoming in that life.

After I shared these images with Joe during his reading, he told me that he'd been a pilot in this life, and his leg problems were so extreme that they prevented him from flying anymore. Again, he'd been relegated to a life on land without command of his craft. Joe now understood that he needed to define himself by the freedom, joy, and well-being that comes from within. This was the key that would release his karma and lead him to a life without restrictions.

I was very happy to share what I saw with Joe, but you don't have to go to a medium to meet your past-life guides and learn what they have to share with you. They're around you whenever you need them, ready to give you glimpses of the histories that are present with you now. All you have to do is call upon them and open your timeless mind and heart to the ever-present and eternal world of your guides.

Chapter 11

TAKING THE PLUNGE

Diving into the deep and sometimes unfathomable waters of eternity can be rather daunting. At the same time, it can be truly exciting and inestimably valuable! And the changes that can result from this adventure will lay the groundwork for a blessed and brilliant future.

The reason we come back is to move forward. The reason we experience pain or pleasure is to learn, feel, understand, and grow. Not every lesson means suffering, but if you find yourself in unpleasant conditions, you might as well learn!

Whatever you may be going through now, your eternal self is capable of clearing the emotional blocks that were constructed in the past. Just as happened for the people in this book, once you understand the issues of your karmic lessons, you're free to completely redefine the direction of your life. It isn't necessary to reverse every past episode, only to construct a new pure and eternal perception.

Your intention to do so can forge a nexus of cause and effect that produces considerable shifts in consciousness and reality. Past, present, and future can transform in the blink of an eye, clearing and redirecting the power of your eternal soul. As you align with your spirit's choices, you'll move into a sacred place where your eternal evolution becomes your own (and perhaps only) motivation.

Fortunes Lost, Fortunes Found

Although much of this book has been devoted to investigating what past problem may be blocking us now, we need to remember that there's plenty of good fortune to go around. Whatever joyous or beneficial experience may come our way, we need to embrace it, acknowledge it, and be grateful. This appreciative attitude toward even the smallest successes in life is a hugely important energy, generating results both in this life and in the time to come. Heartfelt gratitude is always both an immediate and karmic cause, drawing much more to appreciate.

Unfortunately, it's all too common these days for people to focus on what they lack, locking into one issue only—such as money or love. And if that's not satisfying to them, nothing else seems to matter. They ignore the pluses of health, family members, home, hobbies, and all the wonderful little pleasantries they can experience throughout the day. Instead, they filter everything through what's missing, obsessing about romance, money, or success, and spending all their energy lamenting their deficiency.

In terms of karma, this excessive focus on loss can often be traced back to lifetimes that revolve around a *reversal of fortune.* This is where someone has a lot of success, and then it's suddenly ripped away. When it comes to romance, a reversal-of-fortune experience is one of abandonment or betrayal. In these cases, the person never quite gets over the lost love, spending much of that incarnation in longing and misery.

Those energies can become habituated, as was the case with my client Steve. He came to see me to find out what had been blocking his career success, although he'd already achieved a pretty comfortable lifestyle through his landscaping business. He still needed his wife's income in order to put his two kids through college, however; and he felt like a failure if he couldn't do it all on his own. In fact, he'd worked himself up into such a state of longing and self-judgment that he was absolutely miserable.

When we did a focused regression, we went directly to a life long ago where Steve was a very successful landowner in Italy. He had large estates with lush vineyards and even a small functioning military. Unfortunately, in one of the many wars between the regions of that time, he sided with the losing contender. His lands were seized, and he was left virtually penniless. He spent the rest of that existence longing to get his estate back—with no luck.

This experience encoded emotional and cognitive patterns that strongly influenced his life today. First was a longing for greatness that nothing short of extreme success would satisfy. The second code was a surprise to Steve, but it's something I've seen a lot. On a deep and hidden level, my client actually believed that having a lot of money would be unsafe for him. That horrible experience and the poverty it brought about made Steve conclude that wealth would make him a target, and that it would be fleeting and end in some kind of catastrophe.

So he brought into this life both the longing for great wealth and the conflicting intention that he needed to keep his income down in order to stay safe. What a polarity in energy! He now needed to release his desperation for riches and rescript his conclusions, knowing that it would be safe for him to succeed. He used all of the techniques presented in this book and became happier and more satisfied than he'd been in years. And whether it was due to his new, joyful energy or to clearing the karma, his business also began to grow steadily.

When it comes to romance, similar cases of abandonment and loss can cause an unending desperation for love. Oftentimes, the lonely person is obsessed with one specific individual and just can't seem to let the person go. In those cases, it's not unusual to find out that the present object of her unrequited love is the soul who abandoned her in a past life, and the victim is still trying to set things right.

If you find yourself in this pattern of unrelieved longing—whether it be for money, love, or anything else—you need to attack that present negativity. Stop and notice the good fortune you already have. Take some time to list all your blessings, and consciously appreciate them as often as possible. This isn't just New Age claptrap; it's consciousness-changing intention and energy. And as you shift from a *lack* vibration to one of value, you'll go a long way toward healing the karma, too.

Finish releasing the unwanted karmic patterns by using regression to find out their source. Release the pain and longing, and rescript the scenario along with the conclusions. Affirm that you're free from the past, and make it a priority to live your present life in trust and joyous appreciation.

You can use all of the processes on the CD to address any issue from this or other lifetimes. Never forget, however, to recognize and revel in every joyous moment; and take responsibility to create even more happiness each day. By clearing the past and embracing the present, the future is free for you to direct.

How to Use the Enclosed CD

I highly recommend that you read the entire book before listening to the accompanying CD. Since my contributors and I review many cases that demonstrate different people's paths, this will help you facilitate a plan of your own. The processes here have been specifically designed to help take you through the steps described in Chapter 9, so it's a very good idea to read at least that chapter and this one.

Please use the CD at a time when you can thoroughly relax and when you won't be interrupted. Never listen to the guided meditations while driving or trying to engage in activities where you need to be alert. The affirmations can be done within the other processes or on their own.

The affirmations, regression, rescripting, and progression that are on the CD are described here in detail. Please read all of the following sections to familiarize yourself with each purpose and format. Specific suggestions and case studies are given to help you prepare for these important experiential techniques. As you read about each process, consider your intentions. What patterns or relationships do you want to investigate? What present problems do you want to release or heal?

All of the processes are safe, relatively easy, and very purposeful. Let go of your worries and expectations, and trust your spirit to direct you to the information that's most important for your healing and growth. Don't make this harder than it has to be—just relax and be willing to learn. Your higher self longs for you to heal and be happy. Hold that intention deep in your heart as you engage in each process, and you'll be surprised by the wonderful results.

Each meditation includes a visit to your own Sacred Temple. This is a peaceful place where you can relax, connect with spirit—whether yours or others—and get any answers you may need. I've used this Sacred Temple meditation throughout my life; and I recommend that you turn to it whenever you're looking for peace, clarity, or inspiration.

Track 1: Focused Regression

In my opinion, the most powerful and convincing way to access past-life information is through hypnotic regression. When you experience the events and sensations of your former incarnations, you deeply feel the truth; and you can sense how it resonates with your present circumstances.

Some people are extremely uncomfortable with just the idea of being hypnotized. They worry that they're going to lose control or be unable to stop the process if they so desire. They don't realize that hypnosis is just a very deep form of relaxation, a state where brain frequencies move into the alpha-wave frequency, which means that your mind is most open to accessing information and engaging in connections with the energetic realm.

People using hypnotic regression as a way to get past-life information are often concerned about what they'll find out about themselves. They worry that they were "bad" and did horrible things in a past life. They're also anxious about the emotions they'll experience, wondering if they'll be overwhelmed by it all.

But none of these things need be of any concern to you. You're always in control, and you'll always remain so. You can stop the meditation whenever you like, bringing yourself back to the present time and space with ease. The more you realize this, the more you'll be able to relax, which will allow you to be even more receptive to detailed information.

When you do this focused regression, it will usually lead you to an important scene in a previous life. The process on this CD has an induction that takes you back to just a few minutes before the source experience of the issue, problem, or relationship that you want to work on. The information you get can come to you in one of two ways—two different points of view, called *immersion* and *observation.*

Sensing through *immersion* gives you the point of view of actually being within the experience itself. You find yourself in the body and the emotions of the main character—your soul's personality of that time. Since you see things through the eyes of that incarnation, you can look down and see the clothing you're wearing and your hands and feet, but you won't be able to see your face unless you're near a reflective surface such as a body of water or a mirror.

In the case of *observation,* you see the event like a movie playing out in your mind's eye. You'll know which character you are, and you'll be able to watch yourself in the midst of the experience. You can even see what you look like without the assistance of a mirror. Even though you're not in the body you were at that time, there's still an awareness of the circumstances and emotions from the first-person point of view.

In both cases, the information flows freely. Even though you're in a very specific episode from that life, you'll have full memory of everything that happened to you up to that point. For example, you may do a regression in which you receive a letter from your spouse. Even though your partner in that lifetime isn't present, you'll know what that person looks like, what your relationship has been like, and how you feel about him or her.

Both ways of perceiving the past are valid, and there's no indication that the information gleaned in one kind of approach is any truer than the other. There are even some people who don't "see" anything at all. In those cases, they just have a strong sensation of knowing, and their information is just as valid.

The ability to experience all of your senses in a past-life regression will increase with more practice and meditation. The same will be true if you don't get any information at all. Don't fault yourself! Be patient and persistent, and continue to meditate, as well as go through the process on the CD. Over time, you'll find yourself getting more and more sensory input of the information you need.

When you get your information, consider its relevance in your present life. See if you can identify the people in that life in terms of your relationships now. Use a journal to record your impressions, and add any other details that may come up.

When you do a regression, your focus on that past-life issue opens up a portal to more information. So whenever you're in an alpha-wave state after that—whether it's sleeping, daydreaming, or even just performing routine tasks such as driving—you may be surprised to receive very specific information about that past experience, the lesson involved, or how it relates to your present issues.

People often doubt what they discover when doing their first regression. Some think they may just be making it up, assigning the revealed information to some function of their imagination. If this is your response, you need to ask yourself, *Does this resonate with me—especially with respect to emotion, meaning, and conclusions?* If you can figure out the lesson and understand the present application, you need to accept that part of the message as your karmic directive.

In my experience doing regressions and even readings, the information is so vital, so animated, and so completely unexpected that I just can't dismiss it as unfounded imagination. Whether or not we get all the details right, the important thing is the process itself—and the purpose it serves in decoding our past and changing our present

Some people get sidetracked by the information they receive. Those who find out they were victims in a past life sometimes believe they can't change that in the present. They think this pattern must repeat, leaving them powerless in the world today; but really, the opposite is true. The information is given to them so that they can change this code and move out of it once and for all.

Similarly, it can be very difficult to find out that you've done things in the past that would be considered immoral or even criminal today. This kind of revelation can cause some people to go into a deep sense of self-blame. Their guilt can plant a false conclusion that they don't deserve good things in this life because of the bad things they did before.

Never fault yourself for your missteps from the past—it only compounds the karma. You have to realize you did the best you could, given the time, culture, and your own personal history at that time. So forgive yourself! This important information isn't intended to make things worse. It's shown to help you progress into a higher, more enlightened view of things—to raise your self-awareness and empower you in your present life circumstances.

Remember, when it comes to your past lives, it's not that things are good or bad; it's just that the revelation is necessary for your process. In soul terms, there's no success or failure. Your true achievement comes in responding to your lessons with grace, honor, and authentic power.

Track 2: Releasing and Rescripting the Past

The intention in this process on the CD is to empower you in a situation where you may not have felt much power the first time around. You can even rescript episodes from this life, although it may take more repetitions to get the complete results you're looking for.

The format is relatively simple. First, gather your specific past-life information through the guided regression, although you can also rescript scenarios obtained from readings, triggered associations, dreams, or any other method. Consider the events carefully —especially in terms of any unwanted patterns or relationships that you may be able to identify in this life.

In the rescripting meditation, go back to the original event, knowing that your eternal consciousness is now in control. This time, visualize the scene exactly how you want it to go, with a beneficial new ending. Create details showing you taking back your power. Shift the nature and events of the experience, and have the situation work out in a healthy and happy way for you.

At the end, take some time to enjoy the new emotions of empowerment, strength, and value. Then take a deep breath, encoding the new feelings as well as the positive conclusions that go with them. You can use the affirmations from Chapters 8 and 9, or create some of your own. Finally, move forward in that life, visualizing yourself as a healthy, happy, empowered person.

Rescripting can be used in any circumstance. Just turn the details around and see yourself in the newly resolved situation. For example, if you were stabbed in the back in a past life, you can visualize yourself overpowering the person first. You can also hear your attacker, step aside, and escape. Or you can simply turn around and tell the person that it wouldn't be in his best interest to hurt you; then visualize that person agreeing and just walking away.

If you're rescripting an event where you were a child or weak, infirm, or powerless in any way, you can actually see yourself regaining your strength, getting physically bigger and being filled with the power and wisdom you need to handle what's going on.

The purpose of the rescripting is to bring the qualities of your higher self—which is always with you in every event—into that experience. Whether it's wisdom, grace, peace, courage, or any other quality, your intention to bring it to that past event changes both it and you at the core vibration. This erases the code that was imprinted then, stripping away the emotions and the false conclusions along with it. Your rescripting reestablishes the truth that you always have options, bringing a new empowerment to the choices, experiences, and relationships of this life as well.

To prepare for your rescripting, consider the following questions regarding the specific past-life experience you want to revise. It's extremely helpful to write your answers in your journal because it generates the specific intentions you want to encode.

- *What do I need to do to reclaim my power in this situation?*

- *What do I need to express—or even demand—in order to demonstrate my authentic power and my own belief in myself and my value?*

- *What behavior do I need to change in order to restore my health, dignity, integrity, value, power, or peace of mind?*

- *What is the lesson my soul wants me to learn, and how can I change this scenario to achieve that most effectively?*

- *What affirmations can I use to release and reframe this experience?*

Use the answers to these questions to design your rescripting scenario. You'll be given time to see the scene play out exactly as you desire, with a beneficial and empowering outcome. So plan the new narrative ahead of time and get ready to reframe the entire event. The key is becoming aware of the meaning and the lesson of the experience. Only then can you shift the circumstances to serve your healing and evolution.

Realize that patterns of powerlessness and inactivity are just as debilitating as aggression and addictions. Any habit from the past that doesn't nurture you—whether it's brutal physical treatment or stifling relationships—can be rescripted. Find out the connection between the originating experience and your present pattern prisons, then create the intention to heal them both.

Track 3: Future-Life Progression

Just as it's possible to visit the past, you can also get a glimpse into your future potential. Although nothing is predestined, you can take a look at what a life to come might look like, given your present circumstances. You can also examine the interesting realms between the worlds if you so desire.

The intention for "future glimpsing," however, goes back to the purpose of shifting your eternal consciousness. Finding out about the times to come can give you clues about what you need to do in order to deal with the present—and how to do it. This was the case for a client who'd gained a lot of weight after she had her first two children. She was married and enjoyed a happy family life; and although her weight frustrated her, it didn't create any health problems—yet.

When she progressed to a future life, she saw herself as a fat child, a problem she hadn't had to deal with this time around. She saw herself being teased and taunted, depressed and alone, never marrying in that life; and in fact, developing diabetes.

This image shook her and made her want to aggressively deal with the issue now. And although she'd tried diets before, this time she was much more motivated and successful. After she lost weight and shifted her daily habits concerning food, she did another future progression. This time she saw herself in that life to come as a healthy kid, growing up, falling in love, and not having to deal with the challenge again.

This is actually a very common response to future glimpsing. You may only make a brief visit, but that brief impression can really make a difference now and in the time to come. In fact, when you bring a healing intention back from the future, you can change everything!

The process of progression is designed to investigate how present issues influence tomorrow, opening the path to the potential information of lifetimes to come. You'll be able to see or sense the details in ways that you can understand and apply to this existence. This method also features a look into the Akashic Record, the information storehouse that's available to you at all times. Let your doubts go and open up to the images and details that may arrive.

Don't be concerned about what you'll find out in the progression. It's safe and directly related to a current issue that you name at the beginning of the process. If you see something that upsets you even the slightest, you can break into the scene and rescript it immediately. Remember, the future vibrates in future potential and doesn't exist in absolute certainty, so don't take it too seriously. There are so many factors that influence those far-off events, most especially the way you decide to live your life now. *Never forget the power that you have in creating your own destiny.*

Keep in mind that this is an investigative mission to help you with a *present* pattern. This isn't meant to be a process of divination, so you shouldn't use it to find out if you're going to get that promotion, or if the new guy in your building is going to ask you out. The answer to these questions may also be vibrating in future potential, but there are other ways to look into those possibilities.

Future-life progression has a deeper meaning, and when you visit the Akashic Record, you'll find valuable information that can accelerate your present healing. Your honest intention to connect with the related time to come will unlock that door, and your soul will lovingly guide you to the exact information you need. Open your heart to the changes suggested in this experience. You'll be amazed by the sense of liberation and self-mastery you'll be able to achieve.

It's always a good idea to *program future-life intentions*. You can write down those plans; and if you like, you can use them during your meditative progression. I recommend keeping your intentions general, without naming specifics. For example, if I intend to marry my present husband again, it could be contrary to his soul's plan to perhaps come back as a priest. Although the idea of him being celibate may be amusing to me now, a future life of longing for him would cause me great frustration. To avoid problems with the unknown specifics of incarnations to come, I like to word my future-life intentions something like this:

- *In my next life, I will be happy, healthy, and fulfilled. I will be born into a loving and stable family; and I will grow up with encouragement, compassion, and care. I will have a joyous childhood and a long, healthy life.*

- *I will blissfully reunite with the loving and supportive people of the present, and our union will be mutually honoring and joyous.*

- *I will live in a beautiful environment and have abundant wealth. The activities I pursue—whether work, hobbies, or avocations—will be meaningful, enjoyable, and fruitful for me.*

- *My relationships will be rewarding and pleasurable. If I so desire, I will find a wonderful spouse and create a peaceful family; and we will live long, healthy, and happy lives together.*

- *My entire life will be blessed with spiritual, mental, and emotional fulfillment. My body, mind, and soul will receive unending blessings of health, wisdom, inspiration, and enlightenment.*

- *And so it is . . . and so it shall be.*

This is just a sample of what you can intend for the future. I personally don't spend a lot of time focusing on this, but it's worth writing down. It's also a helpful reminder that we can create these peaceful intentions now. We don't have to force our will, but we can keep our minds and hearts open to these ideas. We can consider what inner changes we might make now that would assist in creating a brighter future . . . tomorrow and for all eternity.

Track 4: Karmic-Healing Affirmations

In the old days, when someone used the phrase *to forgive a debt,* it meant that the debt was wiped clean. That's a valuable intention when dealing with unhealthy karmic connections and patterns. The intention is to wipe the slate clean and free yourself from habits of hostility, fear, or unhealthy attachment.

Sometimes when I find myself in a difficult situation, I use these affirmations:

- *I forgive all karmic debt and ask that all my karmic debt be forgiven.*

- *I release any karmic connection or negative attachment to this person, habit, or situation. I am free.*

These intentions of karmic release are especially helpful in situations where others are hostile to you, or you feel anger or resentment toward them. If a relationship seems especially stuck, you can also visualize the beautiful hands of Divine Light bringing golden scissors to sever the threads that bind you, cutting the karma as well as the need to stay connected. As you do this visualization, bless the person and let him go. See the energetic strings being cut, and see the situation—along with the person—drifting peacefully away, making you feel free and healed.

Remember, shifting karma also requires you to release toxic conclusions from past events. These faulty beliefs—the lies of your history, whether from this existence or another—are the biggest source of your present problems. When you arrive at the truth of your value and power in this life, that knowledge can transcend karmic difficulties and heal the energy of all time—past, present, and future.

The following intentions, along with others, are on the CD. Use them to heal both your present and past false conclusions. Your life is a process and never static. Confirm your ability to let go and grow with these releasing and empowering affirmations:

- *I release any negative energy from difficult experiences of the past.*

- *I release any negative conclusions I may have made as a result of those experiences.*

- *I am free and clear of misinformation, and I live in my power and my truth now and always.*

- *I open myself to my spirit's capacity to embrace the full measure of my value, power, and understanding.*

It's Never Too Late for Change

The power of time traveling with intention is truly amazing. It brings to mind a hauntingly beautiful tale that's known throughout the world. In *A Christmas Carol* by Charles Dickens, hard-hearted Ebenezer Scrooge lives a miserly and miserable life. He reluctantly allows himself to be guided by spirits in three revealing trips through time that change him to the very core of his being.

First, he visits the past to see and understand the causes he set in motion there. Then he investigates the present with an awakening realization of the inner patterns he must change. Finally, he goes to the future to see how all these causes play out. When he doesn't like the outcome he sees there, he returns to the present with a deep resolve to reverse the misguided patterns he's been living with for so long.

This is such a beautiful, tender story. It's so brilliantly done that I believe it was channeled by Spirit precisely for the purpose of encouraging us to take a good look at our own past, present, and potential future. No matter what our stuck patterns may be, we, too, can have our own epiphany. In this life-changing awareness, we can realize what we must do and galvanize the will to do it. And if we can resist the temptation to slide back into old habits, we can design a destiny as joyous and revolutionary as Scrooge himself. This is what the soul longs for: to release the blocks of the past, heal the present, and create a truly dynamic future for ourselves and others.

Other Paths to Healing

Although it's informative and sometimes essential to connect with past-life events in order to resolve present issues, it's not always necessary. And you certainly don't have to revisit every occurrence to address every problem. There are many avenues to healing and many ways to clear stuck energy—even from the far-distant past. I'd like to introduce some of them here, and I encourage you to pursue these and other techniques to assist and accelerate any work you're already doing. Whether it's breaking through blockages or bringing resolution to physical, mental, or even financial concerns, your intention to clear old vibrations and open your life to healing energy will help to make it so.

Energy Medicine

One truly powerful approach works with the energy meridians, chakras, and systems of the body. In her book *Energy Medicine*, Donna Eden describes energy as a vital, moving force that can actually determine a person's health and happiness. To achieve and maintain well-being on all levels, it's important for this current to move, to flow in harmony and maintain balance with other systems.

Unfortunately, through stress, conflict, and disturbances both in this and other lifetimes, our energy can become blocked, stuck in a certain chakra, organ, or meridian. Energy Medicine is a noninvasive way to move that stuck stuff out, creating an open channel for our life force to flow and bring healing to the affected area.

You don't have to know the past-life event involved (if there is one) to bring about this kind of healing because it is achieved through many different types of physical and energetic interventions, such as tapping, massaging, tracing meridians, exercises, postures, and mental intentions. You may be surprised, however, by the type of distant memory that comes to the surface when you do this work.

Donna tells the story of a chakra clearing where just such an event occurred. She was working on the heart chakra of an older woman when she saw a past life where this person was a male pianist, who throughout that life had his creative and performance desires stifled. Donna started to tear up from the grief she felt stuck in the heart from that experience; and when she shared what she'd seen, her client started to cry as well. She told Donna that she'd played piano all her life, but because she never felt good enough, she only did so when she was alone. It was a source of sadness for her to keep her talent pent up. Although she'd always been driven by that karmic intention, she was now free to let it go.

I highly recommend Donna's books and seminars if you really want to move old energy out. They're full of specific techniques that are practical and easy to use, and they address myriad problems and conditions. I know these processes have shifted my present vibration and past codes as well.

Energy Psychology

Another extremely helpful way to release stuck patterns is through the use of Energy Psychology, which is especially beneficial in clearing fears, anxieties, and other emotional issues. Once again, it isn't always necessary to know the past-life source because the specific problem has manifested in this incarnation and can be treated in terms of present circumstances as well.

One significant practice of Energy Psychology is the Emotional Freedom Technique (EFT). This process involves tapping on acupressure points to send signals to the brain that change an individual's personal mythology or emotional status. This may seem deceptively simple, but it's an extremely powerful tool. Tapping certain spots while mentally activating a psychological problem can alter the brain chemistry that maintains the dysfunctional response.

For this reason, many people find that Energy Psychology is a remarkably effective and potent way to change the way in which the brain codes emotional and behavioral patterns. In this process, information can come up from the deepest layers of the aura, allowing the release of long-held negative responses and replacing them with healthy perceptions.

In his book *The Promise of Energy Psychology* (with Donna Eden and Gary Craig), David Feinstein, Ph.D., explains the efficacy of this process and relates a number of very successful cases. In one, he examines the complexities of layered information, revealing the potential need for more than one session to break through to the deepest layers.

In that instance, a client was working on emotional healing after a car accident. The anxiety was persistent, however, and in a follow-up session they discovered a sensory aspect. The client described his own accident again, this time adding the element of the smell of burning rubber. He said that when he was five years old, he witnessed a car crash, and that smell was still in his memory.

This old association to his current situation had to be cleared in order to heal the ongoing worry.

In this way, EFT and Energy Medicine can be similar to recoding past-life issues. You may be able to completely heal a deeply emotional or even physical problem with surprising ease and speed. However, you may also find that some issues have to be investigated more thoroughly and addressed more consistently to get the complete resolution you're looking for.

It's well worth the effort when you consider how much your deeply layered concerns influence your life experiences. There are many practitioners of EFT and Energy Medicine; as well as other valuable tools such as acupuncture, massage, Reiki, and therapeutic touch. All of these practices—and many more—help move out old energy and bring balance, vitality, and flow. If any of these or any other techniques resonate with you, let yourself explore their potential assistance in your intention to heal—no matter what issue you may be working on. After all, your soul came here to move forward and to bring balance, enlightenment, and peace to your life in the healthiest ways possible.

Ever in Search of Soul Truth

This is the ultimate purpose of the adventure we call life: *to seek our soul's truth and live in its expression at every opportunity.* It can be difficult, however, to discern exactly what that may mean in any given situation. Whether driven by past-life codes or present challenges, the soul is open to the lesson involved, and our own personality must be willing as well.

I learned this firsthand several years ago when my first book was about to be published. I'd self-published a short version of *Secrets of Attraction* for many years, but when it was to be put out by Hay House, I had to expand on the original and nearly double its length.

When I started the addition, I began having significant pain in my jaw. It moved up into my temples and forehead, giving me debilitating headaches. Every time I tried to write, I was sidetracked by this intense physical response, which made it impossible for me to think. This pattern of jaw pain and chronic headaches went on for several months—*until I decided to do something about it.*

I did a regression to see if there might be a past life involved, and I was amazed by what I found out. Apparently, in the early days of Christianity, I was devoted to spreading the word. I traveled far and wide, preaching the Gospel to anyone who was willing to listen. Interestingly, I was also a woman in that life, and it was rather unusual for a female to be leading such a life. Men had taken over the church and had relegated women to more subservient endeavors.

It became clear in my regression that I'd ruffled the feathers of some local church officials. I was arrested and tried for heresy, where it was determined that I was guilty. To prevent me from ever preaching again, my tongue was cut out. I spent the rest of that life unable to communicate, begging, and surviving off the generosity of others.

That was a very emotional and revealing regression. I remembered the fear and even the physical pain of a knife cutting through to my jaw. I felt the desperation, poverty, and loneliness. And I also recalled the powerful conclusions that it was unsafe for me to express my beliefs, and that any public declaration could only end in catastrophe.

This all came up at a time when I was about to go public with my spiritual views. Although I'd been self-published for years, these past-life conclusions hadn't been stimulated because it had always felt safe for me. But such devastating thoughts couldn't stay quietly coded now that I was about to put myself out there where all could see.

Without even knowing it, I was awash with conflicting intentions. My personal self was excited and wanted to spread my ideas to a wider audience; but my wounded self wanted me to stay safe, even providing the head and jaw pain that would make it impossible to finish the project and get it out there. The lesson was clear: I had to understand that it was safe for me to express my truth.

I worked on releasing the fear, the pain, and all of those false assumptions. I knew that my genuine intention was to let go of the encoded experience that had been keeping me stuck. It occurred to me that it could have been impacting my career in many ways for quite some time. I even wondered how much that old intention to "stay safe" might have influenced my inability to find a publisher for so many years.

But doing that regression set me on a path of conscious intention. I was determined to not only speak my truth from that point onward, but to also try to help others do the same. From the moment I embraced that as my soul's directive, the jaw and head pain disappeared. I never even needed to do a rescripting. I just released the old fear-based code, and I've never had that physical problem again.

This was a very valuable lesson for me. Although the headaches had been difficult, they revealed a deep and abiding personal purpose. My soul wanted me to prioritize expression for myself, and in my work with others. It was liberating to know about that past life, because I never again let fear enter into the equation. Instead, I felt strength and determination filling my communication and expression as never before. That past-life experience no longer restricted me. Now it actually empowered me!

You, too, can be empowered by your past lives—even the difficult ones. You can use the information to enlighten yourself about your options and focus your energy in new and healthy directions. When it comes to your encoded consciousnesses, knowledge truly is power, and it awakens an inner strength that can achieve great things.

Tapestry of Time

Life is richly textured. The dark threads make the brighter hues stand out. Yet even in the darkest places of our eternal tapestry, there is beauty and meaningful detail. We must remember that we are the weavers, bringing color and shading to every experience. Each moment of awareness and heart-driven choice changes the scenes of tomorrow and of all the time to come.

Every incarnation is valuable, every lesson a gift. Good or bad, joyous or sad, all is designed to make your journey better by virtue of the power and enlightenment you arrive at along the way. In your eternal life, you're always in Divine Consciousness. Feel that light flowing within you—from the far-distant past and on into the future—sparking your own present consciousness into healing, balance, and truth.

This is a part of each life lesson: to return your awareness to your eternal truth. Your beauty and value can no longer be denied; for among all your dreams, to acknowledge this is indeed your highest goal. *To live in Sacred remembrance and presence all at once, to feel the Divine Heart beating within your own—these are the eternal truths that make all dreams real.* When you awaken to this dazzling Consciousness within, the unfathomable greatness of your life will unfold; and you'll see that you are capable of wonderful healing, power, and joy.

✳ ACKNOWLEDGMENTS ✳

With love to my family—Sarah Marie Klingler; Benjamin Earl Taylor, Jr.; Sharon Klingler, Vica Taylor; Jenyaa Taylor; Ethan Taylor; Devin Staurbringer; Yvonne Taylor; and Kevin and Kathryn Klingler.

Unending gratitude for the incredible people at Hay House, including Louise Hay, Reid Tracy, Jill Kramer, Jessica Kelley, Jacqui Clark, Nancy Levin, Richelle Zizian, Christy Salinas, Margarete Nielsen, Donna Abate, Anna Almanza, Laurel Weber, and *all* of the other lovely men and women at this wonderful publishing company. And so very much appreciation to the phenomenal team at **HayHouseRadio.com**®, including Emily Manning, Diane Ray, Kyle Thompson, Mitch Wilson, Joe Bartlett, and Rocky George III. You're the best!

For their tireless effort and support, Noreen Paradise, Melissa Matousek, Rhonda Lamvermeyer, and Lucy Dunlap. Thank you!

So much appreciation to my inspiring colleagues: Gregg Braden, Darren Weissman, Eldon Taylor, Lisa Williams, Donna Eden, David Feinstein, Colette Baron-Reid, Peggy McColl, John Holland, Candace Pert, and Mike Ruff.

To the family of my heart—Marilyn Verbus; Barbara Van Rensselaer; Ed Conghanor; Julianne Stein; Melissa Matousek; Tom and Ellie Cratsley; Karen Petcak; Valerie Darville; Esther Jalylatie; and Delores, Donna, and Kathy Maroon—so much love to you all.

To my spirit family—Anna and Charles Salvaggio, Ron Klingler, Rudy Staurbringer, Earl Taylor, Chris Cary, Pat Davidson, Flo Bolton, Flo Becker, Tony, Raphael, Jude, and of course the Divine Consciousness that lives in all things and loves in all ways.

Finally, I want to thank *you* so very much—all of you who have shared your beautiful energy and support in so many ways and have brought so very much value to my life! We may never meet in this life, but we're deeply connected, and I appreciate you more than I can say. May bliss and blessings follow you wherever you go!

✳ ABOUT THE AUTHOR ✳

Sandra Anne Taylor is an internationally renowned speaker, counselor, and consultant who lectures throughout the world on the power of eternal consciousness and personal energy. Her popular radio show, *Living Your Quantum Success,* explores these principles and offers insight, advice, and energy readings to people all over the world. It can be heard Mondays on **HayHouseRadio. com**®.

For more than 25 years, Sandra was a counselor in a private psychology practice, working with individuals and couples in the treatment of anxiety, depression, addiction, and relationship issues. Her Quantum Life Coaching program offers powerful techniques to shift consciousness; heal unwanted patterns; and bring together spirit, mind, and manifestation. Her multidimensional approach brings exceptional clarity and practicality to the science of whole-life healing and personal achievement.

This is Sandra's sixth book with Hay House. *Truth, Triumph, and Transformation* is dedicated to examining all of the myriad influences on attraction, clearing out the fears and misconceptions that have recently become a common reaction to the Universal

Laws. *Secrets of Success,* co-authored with Sharon A. Klingler, explores the holistic and spiritual nature of attraction and manifestation. *28 Days to a More Magnetic Life* is a handy, pocket-sized book that offers daily techniques and affirmations to help anyone shift their energy on a regular basis. Sandra's *New York Times* bestselling book *Quantum Success* is still receiving worldwide acclaim for its enlightening and comprehensive approach to the field of attraction and achievement. Rich in practical application and easy-to-understand principles, *Quantum Success* has been called "the real science of consciousness creation."

Sandra's first book, *Secrets of Attraction,* applies the Universal Laws to the pursuit of love. Her in-depth nine-CD audio seminar, *Act to Attract,* is the first audio program relating the principles of modern science to the experience of romantic attraction.

Sandra has appeared in several movies, including *Beyond Belief* and *The Truth.* She's been interviewed on television and radio all over the world and in many national magazines, including *Cosmopolitan, Woman's World, Family Circle, Redbook,* and *Success;* as well as *New Idea* in Australia. Her books are available in 25 languages and dozens of countries around the globe.

Sandra co-founded (along with Sharon A. Klingler) Starbringer Associates, a speaker and consultant agency that produces audio seminars for personal, spiritual, and business enhancement. For more information—or to schedule lectures, seminars, or private consultations with Sandra—contact her at:

Sandra Anne Taylor
P.O. Box 362
Avon, OH 44011
440-871-5448
www.sandrataylor.net

– or –

Starbringer Associates
871 Canterbury Rd., Unit B
Westlake, OH 44145
www.starbringerassociates.com

❋ NOTES ❋

Hay House Titles of Related Interest

Published and distributed in the Republic of South Africa by: Hay House SA (Pty), Ltd., P.O. Box 990, Witkoppen 2068 • *Phone/Fax:* 27-11-467-8904 info@hayhouse.co.za • www.hayhouse.co.za

Published in India by: Hay House Publishers India, Muskaan Complex, Plot No. 3, B-2, Vasant Kunj, New Delhi 110 070 • *Phone:* 91-11-4176-1620 *Fax:* 91-11-4176-1630 • www.hayhouse.co.in

Distributed in Canada by: Raincoast Books, 2440 Viking Way, Richmond, B.C. V6V 1N2 • *Phone:* 1-800-663-5714 *Fax:* 1-800-565-3770 • www.raincoast.com

✻ ✻

Take Your Soul on a Vacation

Visit **www.HealYourLife.com**® to regroup, recharge, and reconnect with your own magnificence. Featuring blogs, mind-body-spirit news, and life-changing wisdom from Louise Hay and friends.

Visit **www.HealYourLife.com** today!